Building Your Online Store With WordPress and WooCommerce

Learn to Leverage the Critical Role E-commerce Plays in Today's Competitive Marketplace

Lisa Sims

Apress®

Building Your Online Store With WordPress and WooCommerce: Learn to Leverage the Critical Role E-commerce Plays in Today's Competitive Marketplace

Lisa Sims
Conyers, GA, USA

ISBN-13 (pbk): 978-1-4842-3845-5   ISBN-13 (electronic): 978-1-4842-3846-2
https://doi.org/10.1007/978-1-4842-3846-2

Library of Congress Control Number: 2018960389

Managing Director, Apress LLC: Welmoed Spahr
Acquisitions Editor: Louise Corrigan
Development Editor: James Markham
Coordinating Editor: Nancy Chen

Cover designed by eStudioCalamar

Cover image designed by Freepik (www.freepik.com)

Distributed to the book trade worldwide by Springer Science+Business Media New York, 233 Spring Street, 6th Floor, New York, NY 10013. Phone 1-800-SPRINGER, fax (201) 348-4505, e-mail orders-ny@springer-sbm.com, or visit www.springeronline.com. Apress Media, LLC is a California LLC and the sole member (owner) is Springer Science + Business Media Finance Inc (SSBM Finance Inc). SSBM Finance Inc is a **Delaware** corporation.

For information on translations, please e-mail rights@apress.com, or visit http://www.apress.com/rights-permissions.

Apress titles may be purchased in bulk for academic, corporate, or promotional use. eBook versions and licenses are also available for most titles. For more information, reference our Print and eBook Bulk Sales web page at http://www.apress.com/bulk-sales.

Any source code or other supplementary material referenced by the author in this book is available to readers on GitHub via the book's product page, located at www.apress.com/9781484238455. For more detailed information, please visit http://www.apress.com/source-code.

Printed on acid-free paper

This book is dedicated to my late mother who passed away in October 2017. Her passing inspired me to channel my grief in a positive and constructive manner instead of becoming consumed by it. Writing this book became therapeutic for me and helped me as I experienced the different grief stages. Rest in heaven, Ms. Lady. I love you!

Table of Contents

About the Author

Lisa Sims is an Assistant Professor of Web and Mobile Technology for Ashford University's Forbes School of Business and Technology where she teaches technology courses in e-commerce and mobile application development.

Lisa is also the author of six books and the creator and host of The Stretching A Dollar for Entrepreneurs Show on Blogtalkradio.com where she provides money-saving tips for entrepreneurs. She is also the creator and host of The Living To Save Podcast where she helps consumers save time and money while providing a little wisdom for their souls. The following media outlets have interviewed Lisa:

- *Redbook* magazine
- *U.S. News & World Report*
- Huffingtonpost.com
- TheStreet
- Duaihz

Lisa Sims's Social Media Links:

- Facebook: www.facebook.com/stretchingadollar
- Twitter: www.twitter.com/bizmoneysaver and www.twitter.com/authorlisasims
- Instagram: author_lisa_sims
- Stretching Your Cash - www.stretchingyourcash.com

About the Technical Reviewer

Sufyan Bin Uzayr is a writer, teacher, and web developer with over 10 years' experience in the industry. He specializes in a wide variety of technologies, including WordPress, Drupal, PHP, JavaScript frameworks, Python, and UNIX/Linux shell and server management. He is the author of four published books, including *Learning WordPress REST API* (Packt, 2016) and *concrete5 for Developers* (Packt, 2014). He holds four masters' degrees, including one in Information Technology.

Sufyan is associated with various publications, journals, and magazines both in writing and editorial capacity. He is an avid writer and frequently writes about topics related to not just programming and development but also politics and sports. He is also a regular contributor to various academic verticals as an analyst and columnist for topics pertaining to international affairs.

Sufyan is the CEO of Parakozm, a multinational design and development company that offers customized solutions to a global clientele. Parakozm works in the field of embedded software, digital content strategy and consumption, IoT and mobile code solutions, accessible web development, and more. He is also the CTO at Samurai Servers, a web/cloud server management and security company catering mainly to enterprise-scale audiences.

Sufyan takes a keen interest in technology, politics, literature, history and sports. In his spare time, he likes to teach coding and English to young students. He also conducts regular seminars, workshops and classes around the world, especially in India and Central Asia for providing pro bono training and education to needful youth.

Learn more about his works at `www.sufyanism.com`

Acknowledgments

I must first give God all the credit for making this book possible. Without God, I would not have had the book idea along with the strength and perseverance to pursue and write it after my mother's unexpected death. In my darkest hours of grief, God shined His light so that I could see and keep going.

Special thanks and appreciation to Apress for giving me the opportunity to become an Apress author. I appreciate all the dedication and hard work the Apress book team provided throughout the project. All the feedback was invaluable and contributed to bringing this book to fruition. Thank you, Louise Corrigan, James Markham and Nancy Chen, for making it a pleasant and memorable experience along with the technical reviewers who reviewed the content for accuracy.

Most importantly, I want to thank my husband, Timothy, and my two sons, Timothy Jr. and William, for bearing with me as I worked to complete this project. This book illustrates to Timothy Jr. and William that no matter how bad a situation might seem, something good and beautiful can still come out of it as long as you keep the faith and never give up.

Last but not least, thank you for making the investment in your business to reach global online markets by purchasing this book!

Introduction

As an online professor, web developer, and entrepreneur, I understand the theory, methods, and implementation behind e-commerce. Throughout my 20-year career, I helped businesses of all sizes implement e-commerce strategies. Some only had a few product offerings while others had an extensive product inventory that was migrated from a brick and mortar location to an online marketspace only. Over the years, I have observed the technology advances that have made it easier and cost efficient for small businesses to create an e-commerce strategy without breaking the bank.

In today's competitive marketplace, e-commerce for businesses is a necessity. No longer is it considered nice to have. E-commerce has become interwoven into our daily lives just like our need for other basic life necessities such as food and air. How important is e-commerce to consumers? Consumers are willing to pay for an annual Prime membership to shop online with Amazon.com and wait two days for their products to be delivered. I love shopping with Amazon because of the Prime delivery. Who does not like opening their door to find an Amazon box outside waiting?

In years prior to e-commerce, this was unheard of, but today it is commonplace. Why is that? Over the years, consumers' needs have changed. Due to hectic schedules, the prevalence of mobile devices and apps, and the convenience of online shopping, consumers look for businesses that understand this and can cater to their needs. As a business owner, you do not want to miss your opportunity to connect with a global market 24 hours, seven days a week.

WordPress, one of the popular content management systems, is primarily known for its easy blog creation. However, blogging is not its only function. It can also be used to create an online store using various plugins such as WooCommerce, which will be discussed throughout this book.

How can this book help you? Each chapter will walk you through creating your own online store from start to finish. The book's assumption is that you are implementing an e-commerce strategy for the first time with little to no technical experience. Each chapter is written from an entrepreneur's point of view with detailed instructions and illustrations to help set up your online store. It will also share with you some insightful tips that can help you save time and money along the way. You will learn the following:

- The history and evolution of e-commerce

- How to create an e-commerce strategy

- What e-commerce themes are and how to use them

- What WooCommerce is and how it can be used along with WordPress to create your online store

- How to test your online store

- How to secure your online store

- How to market your online store once it is launched

- How to maintain your online store

As you read this book, each chapter will help you customize your e-commerce strategy for your business to maximize your business's success. I know that you will benefit greatly from this book and would love to hear from you. Please feel free to follow me on my social media networks and let me know how you enjoyed the book.

Let's get started.

CHAPTER 1

Introduction to E-commerce

Contrary to what you might think, e-commerce didn't burst onto the scene overnight. It has been around in various forms for years and improves daily. Before we can truly celebrate the present and future e-commerce accomplishments, it's a good idea to look back and review its history.

What Is E-commerce?

Online store. Online payments. Mobile commerce. Chances are if you are reading this book, you are interested in finding out how to implement one or all of these on your website. All of these play a crucial role within e-commerce, but why should you care about them? What impact will these have on you and your business? Everything if you want to stay in business and continue to grow your business's brand. One of the terms mentioned above probably motivated you to purchase this book.

Let's face it. E-commerce is a buzzword that is here to stay and won't be going anywhere anytime soon. Fierce competition exists in the marketplace between businesses for consumers' attention and dollars. They use social media platforms such as Facebook and Twitter along with mobile apps to interject themselves into consumers' lives while trying to influence their buying behavior. No matter how hard you try or what you do, you can't ignore e-commerce. It is not a fad. It's everywhere. From gas stations that accept mobile payments to fast food restaurants that allow us to order online and either pick up or have our food delivered. It is not going anywhere but is also projected to continue to rise in the years to come.

© Lisa Sims 2018
L. Sims, *Building Your Online Store With WordPress and WooCommerce*,
https://doi.org/10.1007/978-1-4842-3846-2_1

Regardless of a company's size, e-commerce needs to be an essential component of it. Why? E-commerce integrated itself into our society and will continue to impact it positively or negatively in some way, shape, or form. Don't think so? Look around your community. How many vacant brick and mortar stores can you count? Unfortunately, the number you counted represents those who succumbed to e-commerce's popularity, availability, and convenience as well as the presence and effects of discount stores such as Walmart. It didn't happen suddenly but gradually.

How did they become a casualty of the retail war? Those businesses followed the traditional business model in which a need is identified, and a store (referred to today as brick and mortar) is opened to address it. As competition from their online competitors increased and consumer buying preferences changed, they tried desperately to compete by offering coupons, discounts, and other marketing items. Many even transitioned from brick and mortar to click and mortar stores. Click and mortar is a type of business model used to describe retailers that allow consumers to shop in-store and online. Stores such as Walmart and Target are good examples of click and mortar. Unfortunately, even with the transition from brick and mortar to click and mortar, many businesses still couldn't survive. They didn't adapt to the changing market conditions as well as their customers' needs soon enough. Likewise, they could no longer deny the elephant in the room: Amazon.

What exactly is e-commerce? People use the terms online shopping, online store, and others interchangeably, but whatever name you use to describe it, there is no denying that it has transformed the consumer shopping experience forever. According to the Pew Internet Research Center, in 2016, 79 percent of Americans made online purchases compared to only 22 percent in 2000.[1] This dramatic increase indicates the tremendous growth, influence, and power of e-commerce on our society as well as on our economy. It also demonstrates the numerous opportunities available for businesses big and small.

E-commerce stands for electronic commerce and can be defined as "the process of buying, selling, transferring or exchanging products, services and/or information via computer networks, mostly Internet and intranets."[2] Although the terms e-commerce and e-business are used interchangeably, they are different. E-business provides a more comprehensive scope of the e-commerce process. E-business includes e-commerce but

---

[1] http://www.pewinternet.org/2016/12/19/online-shopping-and-purchasing-preferences/
[2] Turban, Efrain, David King, Judy Lange. *Introduction to Electronic Commerce*. (New Jersey, 2011, Prentice Hall), 4.

also involves "servicing customers, collaborating with business partners, conducting online learning, and conducting electronic transactions within an organization."[3] Regardless of which term you choose to use, they both involve the buying and selling of products and services over the Internet. Although it might seem that the e-commerce we have come to know and love is a new concept, the foundation began over 50 years ago.

The History of E-commerce

E-commerce originated in the 1960s, but it wasn't the e-commerce we know today. It was known as Electronic Data Interchange (EDI) and allowed businesses to exchange business documents with other businesses' computers.[4] Although business documents were frequently exchanged, the two most common types were purchase orders and invoices. EDI created a standardized format for these business documents that were electronically sent, resulting in a paperless exchange.

During that same period, another advancement occurred as a precursor to e-commerce. During the Cold War, military leaders needed a computer communications system with no central core, location, or base; and one that could not be easily infiltrated and destroyed, leaving the system nonoperational because of an enemy attack. The Advanced Research Projects Agency (ARPA), a division of the U.S. Defense Department, created ARPANET, the first network, used "to connect computers at Pentagon-funded research institutions via telephone lines."[5] ARPANET's purpose was more academic based than military based and allowed more academic institutions to connect to it, providing a far-reaching structure that the military initially envisioned. Why is this important? ARPANET was the first network to use a form of Transmission Control Protocol/Internet Protocol (TCP/IP), which is the industry standard protocol used to connect to the Internet today. Without the invention of ARPANET, the foundation for the network that we now call the Internet would not exist.

---

[3]Turban, Efrain, David King, Judy Lange. *Introduction to Electronic Commerce*. (New Jersey, 2011, Prentice Hall), 4.

[4]https://online.csp.edu/blog/business/history-of-e-commerce

[5]https://www.britannica.com/topic/ARPANET

As we fast forward a decade, new advances in technology steadily continued. In 1970, Videotext, a two-way message service, was researched and developed in the United Kingdom. In 1979, Michael Aldrich, an English inventor and entrepreneur, created the teleshopping concept known as online shopping between businesses and consumers (B2C) as well as businesses and businesses (B2B). During that same year in the United States, online shopping emerged through services such as CompuServe and The Source. In 1981, Thomas Holidays UK debuted the first B2B online shopping system.

Minitel debuted in France in 1982 as an online service making it possible to make online purchases, check market share, search telephone directories, and chat. This was significant because it was the pioneer to the World Wide Web using telephone lines to connect to the Internet. Software and shareware developers used Swreg as an online marketplace to sell their products using merchant accounts. It was founded by Steve Lee and represents one product offered by Digital River MyCommerce in its suite of e-commerce solutions.

We couldn't talk about e-commerce and not mention Tim Berners-Lee's contribution to it. In 1990, Tim Berners-Lee, the British computer scientist, created the first web browser called WorldWideWeb, which allowed us to view the Web on a computer.[6] Four years later in 1994, Netscape unveiled the Netscape Navigator web browser, which then included Secure Sockets Layer (SSL) encryption that helped to encrypt and secure online transactions. One year later, Amazon was created by Jeff Bezos and changed how we purchased books and much more.

Although there has been considerable debate over when the first e-commerce transaction occurred and by whom (due to legality and the lack of money exchange), research suggests that it occurred in 1994 by a 21-year-old man named Dan Kohn. Dan created a website called NetMarket that served as an online marketplace that sold various goods ranging from electronics to jewelry.[7] You can think of NetMarket as the forerunner to the Amazon of today. According to the Smithsonian website, on August 11, 1994, he sold Sting's CD "Ten Summoner's Tales" for $12.48 plus shipping (Amazon Prime didn't exist) to a friend in Philadelphia who used data encryption to secure his credit card information. Even this e-commerce transaction is debatable as the first because another website called The Internet Shopping Network claimed it sold computer equipment one month before Dan sold the CD.[8] Who's on first?

---

[6]https://www.w3.org/People/Berners-Lee/WorldWideWeb.html
[7]https://www.smithsonianmag.com/smart-news/what-was-first-thing-sold-internet-180957414/
[8]https://www.smithsonianmag.com/smart-news/what-was-first-thing-sold-internet-180957414/

E-commerce Today

If you are like most people, when you hear the term "e-commerce" or "online store," you immediately think of the granddaddy of them all: Amazon (Figure 1-1). Before it became the go-to source to find anything and everything, it started out with one purpose: to be an online bookstore. Many questioned whether an online bookstore would succeed because the traditional model involved visiting a physical bookstore to browse and purchase books. Amazon changed not only how people bought books but also how they read them with the creation of the Kindle. The Kindle introduced consumers to electronic books or e-books that could be purchased and read on the device without carrying around physical books. It revolutionized how we read books.

Today Amazon sells not only books but also clothing, electronics, food, toys, health and beauty items, and much more. You name it, and you can probably find it on Amazon. Often, we wonder how we ever made it without them. Amazon represents the Gold Standard of e-commerce that all other online retailers, big or small, are measured against, compete with, and aspire to be. Although Amazon might be the most popular online marketplace that immediately comes to most people's minds, there are other players that have contributed to the e-commerce evolution. One e-commerce marketplace that comes to mind is eBay. Founded two months after Amazon by Pierre Omidyar, an American billionaire entrepreneur, eBay created an online marketplace for consumer-to-consumer and business-to-consumer transactions. If people could not find what they were looking for on Amazon.com, they could search for it on eBay as well as sell items. With its PayPal integration for online payments, businesses and consumers felt comfortable using the website. In Chapter 4, eBay's history will be discussed a little further.

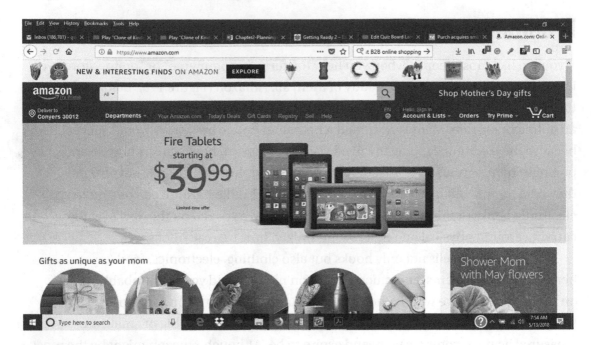

Figure 1-1. *Jeff Bezos formed Amazon on July 5, 1995*

In 1999, Alibaba was founded by Jack Ma. It is considered China's and possibly the world's biggest e-commerce company. According to the *Wall Street Journal*, Alibaba transactions on its three websites (Taobao, Tmall, and Alibaba.com) were estimated to reach $713 billion last year, surpassing both eBay and Amazon.com combined.[9] In the same year, Sky Dayton and Jake Winebaum founded business.com. Business.com not only provided information and resources for small businesses but also provided a marketplace for business products and services.[10] Purch, a digital marketing company, later acquired business.com.

Everyone loves getting a deal and Groupon.com does not disappoint (Figure 1-2). It was established as a "deal-of-the-day recommendation service for consumers."[11] These "deals" are typically deeply discounted, saving consumers money. Whether consumers use the Groupon website or the app, they can use the free service to find travel destinations, products, and services discounts from merchants located in over 15 countries.

---

[9]http://projects.wsj.com/alibaba/

[10]https://techcrunch.com/2016/06/22/purch-acquires-business-com/

[11]https://www.lifewire.com/how-does-groupon-work-2483270

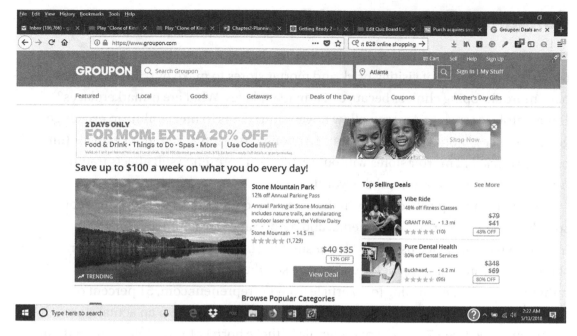

Figure 1-2. *Groupon.com was founded online in 2008*

Before 1995, consumers relied heavily on physical stores for their everyday needs. In e-commerce terminology, physical stores are also referred to as brick and mortar stores. Many of these brick and mortar stores were near their homes or in surrounding communities and carried the items they needed. Consumers could see and touch the items and immediately purchase them, resulting in instant gratification. Once the purchase was over, the relationship between the business and the consumer ended until the next visit or items were returned. This is also referred to as a business-to-consumer (B2C) model, which most of us are familiar with due to our own consumer experiences. You will learn more about the different e-commerce business models in Chapter 2. However, on certain occasions, these items were out of stock. When these items were out of stock, they either drove to another location, had the items ordered from another location by the first store they visited that was out of stock, or waited until it was back in stock. Depending on the item's popularity, it could take a while, which would lead to frustration and dissatisfaction.

Consumer Behavior and E-commerce

Since 1995, technology has steadily advanced to the point that what was once a dream is now a reality. Instead of visiting brick and mortar stores to make purchases, consumers have more shopping choices because of e-marketplaces. What are e-marketplaces? E-marketplaces such as Amazon allow buyers and sellers to meet online to exchange goods, services, money, or information.[12] Although Amazon is an e-marketspace (and opening brick and mortar stores without cashiers), its presence still affects traditional brick and mortar stores around the world.

Due to technological advances in the areas of e-commerce, Internet connection speeds, Internet security, social media, and mobile app development along with increased mobile device usage and faster shipping options, consumers have more shopping options than ever before. There are still those that prefer to shop in-store rather than online. According to an article from Entrepreneur.com, 51 percent of Americans prefer e-commerce, and 49 percent prefer heading into an actual store.[13] It also mentioned that 67 percent of millennials (those born between 1983 and 2000) prefer to shop online versus in-store.

Consumers have less disposable income to spend and want to make sure they are getting the best deals possible. They use price comparison apps on their mobile devices while shopping in-store and use price comparison browser add-ons and extensions when shopping online. Brick and mortar retailers often miss out on potential sales because their prices are not as competitive with those for similar items online.

With the new shift in how consumers shop, many brick and mortar stores who are not shifting their business models as economic conditions and consumers' needs change have either gone out of business or are slowly going out of business. Other factors that contribute to them closing their doors include convenience, flexibility, and popularity of e-commerce. Consumers value their time and money and e-commerce caters to both. Instead of visiting a brick and mortar store to purchase items, consumers are using the power of the Internet and their mobile devices to shop for goods and services while avoiding crowds, long lines, and limited product selections. With a press of a button, they can have their items delivered to their doorsteps or to a brick and mortar store to avoid shipping costs.

---

[12]Turban, Efrain, David King, Judy Lange. *Introduction to Electronic Commerce.* (New Jersey, 2011, Prentice Hall), 6.

[13]https://www.entrepreneur.com/article/306678

E-commerce in Big and Small Businesses

Believe it or not, there was a time when e-commerce was only available to large companies. Why is this? Setting up e-commerce was expensive and involved a great deal of technical expertise. Depending on the amount of inventory available to sell, it could also be time consuming. Big businesses had the in-house technical and marketing expertise along with more extensive budgets to purchase the necessary resources and equipment to either do it themselves or hire consultants to do it. Some of these resources consisted of hardware, software, and personnel (internal and external). As hardware and software updates became available for the e-commerce components, big businesses could readily purchase them to not only keep their operations going but also enhance them.

In the past, when it came to small businesses, it was unfortunately a different story. Small- to medium-sized businesses operated with a handful of employees doing multiple jobs to cut costs and lacked the financial resources to purchase the necessary e-commerce components to compete with their big business counterparts. Due to the nature of their size, small businesses' expenses were typically higher. They also lacked the internal technical expertise to do it themselves along with the money to hire a consultant. Sometimes they relied on friends and volunteers to help fill those technical and staffing voids, which wasn't always the best idea. As a result, they were either forced to abandon the idea of an e-commerce solution or implement it on a tiny scale because of limited resources. This might describe your business, but things are about to change.

Why E-commerce?

Now that you know you can create an online store, the next question becomes why should you create one? Which of the following accurately describes you and your business?

- You own a brick and mortar store and are considering adding an e-commerce component to become a click and mortar store where people can purchase in-store and online and have items shipped directly to them or your store.

- You own a brick and mortar store but want to close it and sell strictly online.

- You plan to launch an online store only to sell physical or digital products or services or both.

9

When it comes to e-commerce, most people have the *Field of Dreams* fantasy where they believe that if they build and launch an online store, customers will come. If only it was that simple and easy! It is always good to dream big but be realistic at the same time. Contrary to popular belief, e-commerce requires a lot of planning and work. No matter how well you design your e-commerce store, potential customers might never visit or make a purchase. On the other hand, your sales might not be as high as you anticipate. These are the realities that you must plan for.

Don't let me scare you! E-commerce is not all doom and gloom. Depending on your purpose, e-commerce has its benefits.

Some of them include:

- Sell your products or services to a global audience.

- Reduce overhead costs such as rent, utilities, and salaries due to doing business over the Internet.

- Sell physical or digital products and services.

- Unrestricted store hours, which allows you to sell 24/7.

- Create and maintain your own store without paying expensive consultants to do it.

- Sell to customers on any Internet-connected mobile device.

- Improve customer service.

- Setup is quicker and easier than a brick and mortar store.

Whatever reasons you have for adding e-commerce to your business model, always remember that first and always you will be in the people business. Without people with a need for your products or services, you won't have a business nor a need to sell online.

With all its advancements and advantages, e-commerce has leveled the playing field by eliminating many barriers to entry that once existed and kept many businesses out. Today, anyone or any sized company can set up an online store with relative ease with low cost and efficient technology such as WordPress and WooCommerce. No matter what tools you use, your online store will only be as good as your plan. The same way you shouldn't build a house without a blueprint, you should not create an online store without one. Planning is essential. As the old saying goes, "If you fail to plan, you plan to fail." The rest of this book aims to help you develop a plan and show you how to execute your plan. In the next chapter, you will learn why it is vital to create an e-commerce strategy and how to go about creating one.

Open Source Software

Regardless of the size of your business and budget, innovations in technology have now made more e-commerce solutions available and affordable. One of these innovations is open source software. Open source software refers to "any program whose source code is made available for use or modification as users or other developers see fit. Open source software is usually developed as a public collaboration and made freely available".[14] What does this mean? With open source software, the underlying program or source code that you don't see with commercial software such as Microsoft Office is made available to anyone to change without restrictions. Commercial software, on the other hand, provides a per computer license price or fee and doesn't allow changes to its source code. Other rules govern open source software, but for our purposes you just need to know it provides us with a license to use, change, and distribute it freely. There are so many open source software options to choose from, particularly with e-commerce. You can think of open source software as your own do-it-yourself toolkit that keeps costs down while providing the same comparable functionality as commercial software that larger companies use.

When open source software became available in 1998, people were skeptical about it not being equal with more well-known commercial software from well-known and established vendors such as Microsoft. They were also concerned about functionality, reliability, and security. Twenty years later, open source software is still going strong and growing by leaps and bounds.

One of the most popular open source do-it-yourself (DIY) open source blogging platforms that we will discuss in latter chapters that will help you implement your e-commerce solution is WordPress. WordPress is a free content management system (CMS) with free and premium themes that can be used to create professional websites and blogs without requiring a web design background, resulting in a low cost of maintenance and ownership. Its core functionality can also be extended by choosing from a selection of free and premium plugins and scalable enough to grow as a business's needs grow, which reduces the need to purchase another system. How popular is WordPress? According to Forbes.com, WordPress powers 30 percent of all websites from hobbyists to the biggest news sites online.[15] Whatever features you want to add to your website or blog, they are probably already available within WordPress via the click of a button, and support is readily available from WordPress.org, blogs, YouTube, and podcasts.

---

[14]http://whatis.techtarget.com/definition/open-source
[15]https://www.forbes.com/sites/montymunford/2016/12/22/how-wordpress-ate-the-internet-in-2016-and-the-world-in-2017/#cfd30bb199d9

WordPress and WooCommerce are not the only options that can be used to create online stores for small businesses. Another popular solution that appeals to small businesses is Shopify. Unlike WordPress and WooCommerce, Shopify is a proprietary online and retail e-commerce solution. What does that mean? Users cannot modify the source code and will have to wait for the company to add new and updated features that might involve an additional cost. Another e-commerce option is Prestashop. Unlike Shopify, Prestashop is open source and can be installed on a web host that supports it. It offers similar features as most e-commerce solutions but requires a little more technical knowledge to extend its functionality. Likewise, it was designed for medium and enterprise-sized businesses. Some other options available are:

- Volusion

- Magento

- osCommerce

- OpenCart

- PayPal

For this book's purpose, we will discuss WordPress and the e-commerce solution, WooCommerce, in Chapters 3 and 4.

Summary

This chapter presented an overview of e-commerce along with its history. It also examined consumers' behaviors toward e-commerce and why small businesses should consider implementing it. The next chapter will discuss some key components to planning a successful e-commerce strategy for your business.

CHAPTER 2

Planning Your E-commerce Strategy

In the previous chapter, you gained a better understanding of e-commerce and its impact on local and global economies as well as local businesses. E-commerce retailers such as Amazon.com, eBay, and Walmart.com have dominated the virtual marketspace and changed how consumers shop and how enterprises conduct business. You also learned more about its history than you probably wanted to know, but it helped you understand the foundation upon which the e-commerce that we know today is based. After reviewing its history and its current state, there is no denying that advances in technology have brought us to a place many never thought was possible. By now, you probably have already determined that you need to add e-commerce to your business, but you still might be unclear as to how to do that. Where should you begin?

Why Create an E-commerce Strategy?

The appeal of e-commerce's low startup costs, ease of entry, and potential profits can make anyone want to immediately launch a web page with some PayPal "Buy" buttons on it and begin selling products and services online. Although this approach might yield some short-term sales, it might not be as successful in the long term. Why? It wasn't based on a solid foundation that was well thought out and will eventually fail. Does the saying, "If you fail to plan, you plan to fail" ring a bell?

© Lisa Sims 2018
L. Sims, *Building Your Online Store With WordPress and WooCommerce*,
https://doi.org/10.1007/978-1-4842-3846-2_2

When deciding to implement an e-commerce strategy, planning is crucial (Figure 2-1). It allows you to take an eagle-eye view of your company and its products and services to determine the best way to present and sell them to your target audience. It also helps determine whether your products or services would be a good fit to sell online. Even though technology gives us the ability to create online stores to sell anything to anyone doesn't necessarily mean that we should. Some things don't sell well online. As a result, money and time are wasted trying to entice people to buy things that don't interest them when it could have been better used elsewhere.

So, what makes a good plan? Before the days of global positioning systems (GPS) in cars and on mobile devices, we used good old-fashioned maps or an atlas to help guide us to our destinations. We'd unfold it, spread it out, and chart our course by identifying our starting as well as ending location. As we drove along, we would review the map to verify that we were traveling in the right direction before we veered too far off course. If we found ourselves lost, we would either pull over and look at the map again or ask for directions (depending on your sex). Once we were back on track, we felt confident and assured that we would reach our destination.

The same way that you would use a map or GPS for a trip, your e-commerce strategy would be your map. It will guide you to your end goal so that you can be successful. Along the way, you might venture off course, but you can always review your strategy and make the necessary corrections to get back on track. The good thing about your approach is that it not only meets your current needs, but it also anticipates and grows with your future needs. This is called scalability. According to Techopedia.com, scalability is "an attribute that describes the ability of a process, network, software or organization to grow and manage increased demand." For instance, you might only have physical products to sell right now, but what if you want to sell digital products? Did you plan for this? Could your e-commerce solution handle this? These are the types of things that your strategy can help you identify so that you can acquire the necessary resources. A good strategy or plan is never complete. It is always a work in progress that must continuously be reviewed and updated.

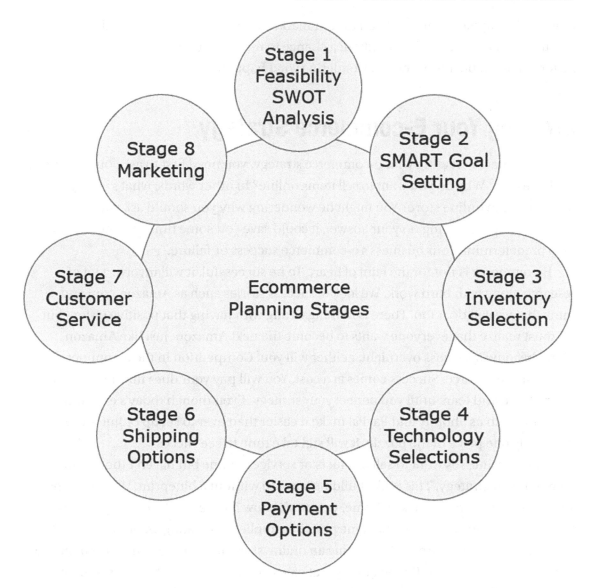

Figure 2-1. *E-commerce Planning Stages*

Planning your e-commerce strategy also helps your business adapt to changing market conditions so that you can stay competitive. Within the e-commerce marketspace, competition is fierce and continuously evolving. Many brick and mortar businesses are steadily transitioning themselves into click and brick stores. Click and brick stores have physical store locations but also offer customers the ability to shop online and have items either shipped to their homes or picked up at a store location. Trends change so rapidly that you must stay well-informed of what is going on in the market to compete for and hold on to your market share. Otherwise, you and your business could get left behind without a chance to recover. Before you know it, you could be forced out of business and left wondering what happened.

Creating Your E-commerce Strategy

Before you begin creating your e-commerce strategy, you need first to ask yourself one vital question: Why do you want to sell items online? In other words, what's your purpose for creating an online store? You might be wondering why you should ask yourself this question, but depending on your answer, it could save you some time and money and help predetermine your business's e-commerce success or failure.

E-commerce is not for the faint of heart. To be successful, it will involve a lot of research along with hard work. We look at success stories such as Amazon.com and think that we can do it too. There is nothing wrong with having that positive vision, but we must realize that everyone wants to become the next Amazon. Just like Amazon didn't become a success overnight, neither will you. Competition in the e-commerce marketspace is fierce. Success comes at a cost. You will pay your dues through trial and error, sweat, and tears until you perfect your strategy. Even though today's e-commerce solutions such as Shopify and PayPal make it easier than ever to set up online stores, that's only one piece of the puzzle. It will still take time to see success.

Many businesses want to sell products or services online but haven't thoroughly planned their strategy. This is like building a house without a blueprint. Who does that? Even though you might make a home, you don't know if it was built correctly or how long it will remain standing. The same principle applies to creating an online store. By understanding your purpose for starting an online store, it will keep you focused on your end goal and not just profits. Not to say that gains are not essential, but to keep them consistently flowing, you must be diligent.

SWOT Analysis

Your next step will involve taking a high-level, objective look at your business and its internal and external processes. By doing this, you will be able to discover the feasibility of e-commerce for your business. Just because you can create an online store does not always mean that it is in your best interest to do so. An excellent tool to help determine this is a SWOT Analysis. A SWOT Analysis is a study undertaken by an organization to identify its internal strengths and weaknesses as well as its external opportunities and threats. For instance, if you are a brick and mortar or click and mortar store, e-commerce will more than likely be an additional sales channel for your business, which can represent an opportunity. On the other hand, if you will be conducting all your e-commerce online, you will be considered a pure-play organization that can represent many strengths such as low overhead costs. Regardless of your business's type, it is crucial that you learn about your business through your SWOT Analysis so that you can plan your strategy around it (Figure 2-2). If you search for SWOT Analysis in Microsoft Word, you will find a free PowerPoint and Microsoft Excel template. You can also Google to find many free step-by-step articles and tutorials.

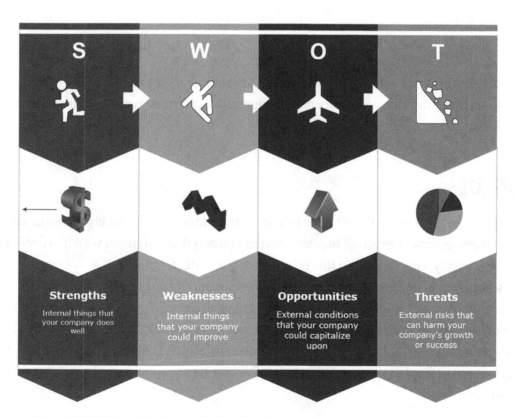

Figure 2-2. *SWOT Analysis can help plan your e-commerce strategy*

Goal Setting

How will you know if your online store is a success or not? If you are like most people, you will probably say, "by looking at the volume of sales." Although this is important, it is not the only measure of success. In addition to having an end goal, you will want to create some other goals to help evaluate your progress and success. We've all heard the saying, "A goal without a plan is just a dream," and to have a positive return on investment (ROI), you need to establish some goals. As with any goals, they need to be SMART:

- Specific

- Measurable

- Attainable

- Relevant

- Timely

These criteria will help you evaluate whether your goals are realistic or whether they need to be revised. Once you have created your goals, you must review them periodically to make sure that you are still on track.

Budget

Wouldn't it be great if you didn't have to worry about money? Absolutely! Unfortunately, being an entrepreneur or small business owners means that you must watch every dollar and use it wisely. One way to do this is by creating a budget.

Establishing a budget is another critical component of your online store. We've all heard that it takes money to make money, but until you can get it flowing into your business on a consistent basis, you will want to create and stick to a budget. Although we will be using WordPress as our e-commerce solution, which is open source software and free, there are still other expenses that you might not be aware of that you will need to budget for such as:

- Web Hosting

- Domain Name

- SSL Certificate

- E-commerce Theme

- E-commerce Plugins

- Marketing tools and materials

- Search engine optimization

- Merchant account and fees

- Credit card fees

- Employee costs

- Warehouse space (if applicable)

- Analytics software to track visitors and their movements on your store

Of course, there will be more, but these are just a few to get you started. By being aware of them ahead of time, they won't come as such a surprise when they occur. You will already be mentally and financially prepared. Throughout the book, we will discuss many of these budget items in detail.

Inventory

An online store is only as good as the items that it sells and who knows your catalog better than you. You probably already have a pretty good idea of the things that you want to sell. Typically, they will fall into one or all of these categories:

- Physical products

- Services

- Digital media

Offering physical products allow consumers to see images of the item before making a purchase. They also require shipping. From a business standpoint, you must determine which shipping methods will be used, along with the cost. You also must decide where you will store the products until they are purchased. If you operate a brick and mortar or click and mortar store, you already have inventory storage available. However, if you are a pure-play retailer, you will have to find a room, which could involve additional costs. With services, you don't have to worry about storing or shipping anything. Services are intangible, so the only thing that needs to be provided is the service.

Since mobile technology has made the shift to digital media products and services more accessible to retrieve and receive, you should determine whether your product offerings will consist of digital products, physical products, or a combination of the two. Based on your knowledge of your customer base, you should be able to decide.

Timeline/Project Schedule

In the IT field, whenever you ask someone, "What's the deadline for this project?," the answer was always "yesterday." When it comes to launching your online store, you might feel the same way. However, if you want to make sure it is done the first time correctly, you will need a project plan or schedule. Otherwise, you can end up spending more time and money than you originally anticipated.

Most people think of Microsoft Project when they hear the words "project plan." Although it is a useful project management tool with many advanced features and capabilities to use to plan your project, it is typically used in larger companies for larger projects. Occasionally, it can be overkill for smaller projects, especially if you don't know how to use it correctly. Not to mention that there is also a learning curve that goes along with it that you don't need while creating your online store. You need a simple way to record all the necessary tasks, their estimated duration and along with their start and end dates, and the person assigned to them. Depending on the size of your business, the person designated could be solely you or other people, but at least you will know. Some free and low-cost tools for creating your project schedule include:

- Microsoft Excel

- Libre Office Calc

- Google Sheets of GSuite

- Zoho.com

- Trello

- Basecamp

- Asana

Other online project management software can be found by Googling. Likewise, mobile apps can be found in Apple's App Store or Google's Play Store. It doesn't matter what application you use if you are comfortable with using it.

Once you have all your project tasks recorded, you will be able to determine a projected completion date for your online store. This date is not set in stone but gives you an idea of your potential time frame. Your project plan now becomes your road map and will guide you to the finish line. This plan must be reviewed and updated periodically to reflect your project's progress accurately. Otherwise, it is an ineffective tool.

Things to Consider

During the planning phase, it is not uncommon for some requirements to get overlooked. These oversights can make a big difference and could negatively affect your bottom line. If you are not careful, they could even cost you extra money, which could affect your budget. Here are some items for you to consider as you think about your online store.

Online Store Planning Checklist

- Have you purchased a domain name?
- How much have you budgeted for web hosting?
- What payment gateway will you use?
- Will you need to acquire an e-commerce theme for your store?
- Is your e-commerce theme responsive or mobile ready?
- Will you need an online merchant account?

Target Audience

- Who is your target audience?
- How will you attract your target audience?

Product/Service Selection

- Will you offer digital or physical products or both?
- How many products or services will you start with?
- How often will you update product or service offerings?

Customer Service

- How will you handle customer service issues?

- What will be your refund policy?

- What will be your privacy policy?

Marketing

- How will you market your online store?

- What techniques will you use for customer retention?

These are not all the questions you will ask, but at least these will get you started. In the next chapter, we will take a look at WordPress and how it can help you start to build your e-commerce strategy and solution.

Summary

Planning is the cornerstone for any effective and successful e-commerce strategy. No one builds a house without a blueprint, and no one should build an online store without a plan. Nothing good ever comes from haphazardly creating an e-commerce strategy. Short-term results might be achieved, but for long-term results, a solid plan is a must. Other planning components that should be considered include:

- SWOT Analysis

- Goal Setting

- Inventory Selection

- Timeline/Project Schedule

By considering these components before launching an online store, you minimize the chances of wasting time and money.

CHAPTER 3

Overview of WordPress

WordPress? What in the world is it? What do you do with it?

You might have heard of it but still have no clue as to what it is, what it does, and how it can benefit you and your business. Not to mention where to get it. That is until now. WordPress has quickly become a game changer in the lives of many entrepreneurs, small business owners, and others seeking a cost-effective web presence.

What Is WordPress?

In nontechnical terms, WordPress is "open source software you can use to create a beautiful website, blog, or app."[1] By being open source, it is free to use, modify, and distribute the software according to the GNU General Public License (GPL).[2] According to the GNU website, the GNU Public License "is a free, copyleft license for software and other kinds of work". the GNU General Public License is intended to guarantee your freedom to share and change all versions of a program – to make sure it remains free software for all its users.[3] At the time of this book's writing, the current version is GPL v3. Compared to proprietary software such as Microsoft Office whose source code is closed and only available to the original creators to modify, open source software empowers users to freely make changes to the source code anytime and share them with anyone. If a feature is missing or needs to be added, users who are technically astute can add it by modifying the source code.

---

[1]https://wordpress.org/
[2]https://opensource.org/licenses/gpl-license
[3]https://www.gnu.org/licenses/gpl-3.0.en.html

© Lisa Sims 2018
L. Sims, *Building Your Online Store With WordPress and WooCommerce*,
https://doi.org/10.1007/978-1-4842-3846-2_3

WordPress is a content management system. A content management system (CMS) is a software application that provides the capabilities for creating, organizing, editing, and publishing content to the Web.[4] Instead of requiring multiple software applications, only one application is required. According to WordPress.org, WordPress is used by 30 percent of the websites and blogs on the Web, ranging from hobbyist to mainstream online news sites.

Some of the companies that use WordPress to power their websites and blogs include:

- The Obama Foundation

- Angry Birds

- TechCrunch

- Pulse by Target

- Bloomberg Professional

- Vogue India

- BBC America

- Tribune Media Group

- Georgia State University (my alma mater)

Not only is it robust enough to work for a solopreneur, but it is also scalable enough to handle the needs of an enterprise organization.

Prior to WordPress, when a business wanted a website created, it either used a web designer within its company or hired a web designer consultant. Due to the lack of technical expertise in-house, most small businesses were either forced to hire an external consultant or freelancer or find a volunteer looking to gain some website design experience to create one. While already working with limited resources and budgets compared to bigger businesses, creating a small business website could quickly become an expensive undertaking depending on the website features. Once the website is launched, it will need to be maintained and modified, which is an additional expense. A simple informational website can quickly become expensive. How can WordPress help?

---

[4]http://www.wpbeginner.com/glossary/content-management-system-cms/

WordPress Popularity

Googling the phrase "creating a blog," WordPress appears in many of the search results displayed on the first page of the search-engine results page. With all the open source and proprietary content management systems available, why is WordPress so popular? Since its release in 2003, WordPress has continually added new features to help entrepreneurs, small- and medium-sized businesses, universities, and others successfully achieve their website goals. Here are just a few reasons why WordPress's popularity continues to grow.

Intuitive User Interface

As mentioned previously, WordPress empowers average users with little to no web design or technical expertise to create beautiful websites and blogs. It is almost like having your own web designer in a box. With its very intuitive and easy-to-use dashboard, pages and posts can be easily created (Figure 3-1).

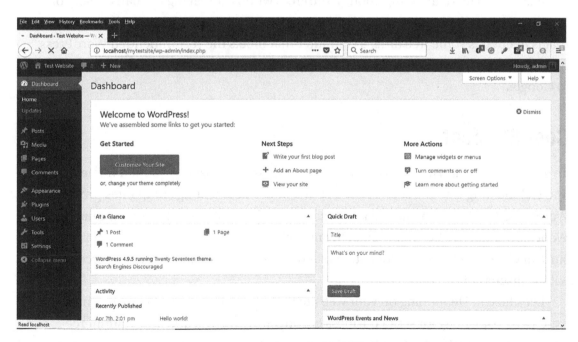

Figure 3-1. *WordPress Dashboard where users create and modify their websites*

Free and Low-Cost Training Resources

With many free and low-cost training resources available on the Web, anyone with a desire to learn WordPress can learn it. Regardless of a person's learning style, helpful resources are available. Some of these WordPress resources are available in the following forms:

- Online courses

- Webinars

- YouTube videos

- Podcasts

- Blog articles

- WordPress.org Codex (online WordPress manual)

- Books

It is easy to learn anything about WordPress without breaking the bank. Many of these options will allow anyone to learn anytime, anywhere, and on any device. All that is needed is some free time, a computer that meets the recommended WordPress requirements for installing WordPress website with administrator rights, and the ability to Google.

Cost Efficient

To get started using WordPress to create a commercial website, a domain name and web hosting is required. As stated earlier, most web hosting companies provide WordPress hosting via a one-click installation at affordable monthly and annual rates. WooCommerce will be discussed in the next chapter and used to create a sample online store in Chapter 7. Other needed items such as SSL Certificate and e-commerce themes will be discussed.

Let's face it. Depending on your website design needs, web designers can be expensive, especially for small businesses budgets. Once you add an e-commerce component, it can become even more expensive. Don't believe me? According to an article on Elegantthemes.com, the average hourly rate for a WordPress Developer ranges from $20 to $100 per hour.[5] If you consider that even a simple online store with 10 products can take 10–25 hours to set up, you can easily expect to pay between $200 to $2,500. WordPress can help businesses save money on their website needs.

Easy Setup and Maintenance

With its easy-to-use interface, a blog, website, or online store can be set up quickly. For creating online stores, the more information prepared ahead of time, the quicker a store can be up and running. Need to add more products or services? No problem! WordPress allows multiple user logins to be created with various permission levels that can be used, too. It can also be manually updated to the latest version (Figure 3-2) or set to update automatically.

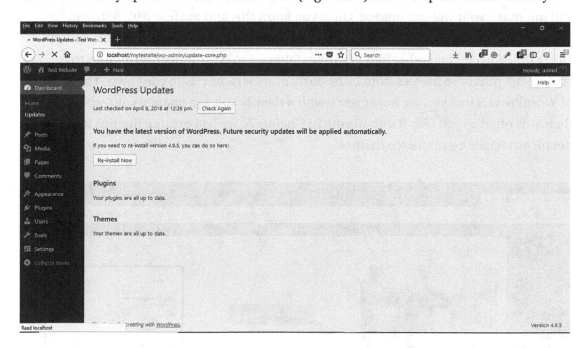

Figure 3-2. *WordPress Dashboard option for WordPress Updates*

Themes

What are WordPress themes? In simple terms, a theme is the outward appearance of your website that your target audience sees. It also helps make a good first impression. In other words, a template is a predefined file where you can insert images and other

---

[5]https://www.elegantthemes.com/blog/resources/heres-the-average-wordpress-developer-salary-is-it-fair

necessary web content into designated placeholders. WordPress.org's Codex defines a theme this way:

> A collection of files that work together to produce a graphical
> interface with an underlying unifying design for a weblog. These
> files are called template files. A Theme modifies the way the site is
> displayed, without modifying the underlying software.

Once installed, WordPress contains several free themes available to use (Figure 3-3). Not sure how a theme will look on your website, blog, or online store? You can preview a theme before activating it. However, there is one caveat concerning using the standard WordPress themes to keep in mind: someone else might use the same theme, which will not make your website unique. Once you know this and are fine with it, use it! You can still change the colors and other theme parts to customize it. Still concerned? Don't fret! You can find other free WordPress themes at WordPress.org/themes to customize, purchase themes from third-party providers, or create your own. The beauty of WordPress is that you are never stuck with a theme. You can change your website's theme as often as you like. It's up to you. In Chapter 5, we will explore themes in more detail, especially e-commerce themes.

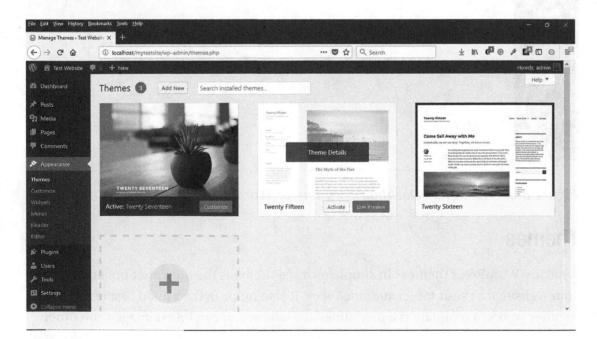

Figure 3-3. *WordPress themes can be selected or added on the Themes page.*

Plugins

Ask any WordPress user or developer, and he or she will tell you that plugins are the heart and soul of WordPress; but what are they? Plugins are ways to extend and add to the functionality that already exists in WordPress (Figure 3-4).[6] In other words, you don't have to re-create the wheel because more than likely someone has already created what you want to do. For instance, if you want to add e-commerce to your website, you can add the WooCommerce plugin through the WordPress Dashboard. All you need to do is configure its settings. How simple is that?

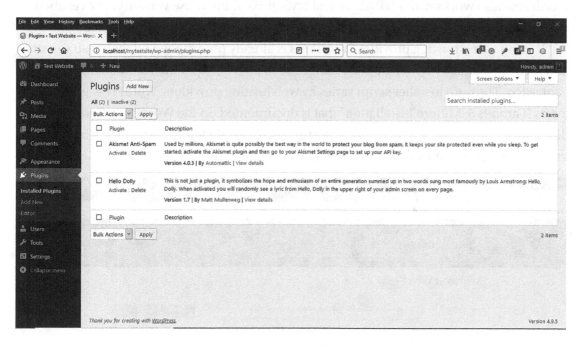

Figure 3-4. *WordPress Plugins that are installed and can be added*

WordPress empowers users to add needed functionality to their websites at their convenience.. Not sure where to find plugins? Many free plugins are available at wordpress.org/plugins. As of the writing of this book, there are 54,860 plugins available from wordpress.org. This number will continue to increase. You'll become more familiar with installing the WooCommerce plugin and others when we start installing WooCommerce in Chapter 5.

---

[6]https://codex.wordpress.org/Plugins

Where to Get WordPress

WordPress is available for download to install on your own web server or local computer from the official WordPress website, `www.wordpress.org/download` (Figure 3-5). It is a good idea to review the recommended WordPress requirements before downloading and installing it. Although PHP version 7.2 or greater and MySQL version 5.6 or greater or MariaDB version 10.0 or greater are recommended, WordPress can be installed on older environments. The WordPress.org website offers this advice about using "legacy environments."

If you are in a legacy environment where you only have older PHP or MySQL versions, WordPress also works with PHP 5.2.4+ and MySQL 5.0+, but these versions have reached official End of Life and as such **may expose your site to security vulnerabilities**.[7]

If using a web hosting provider, WordPress is already preinstalled on their web servers and ready to install with a single click using auto installer scripts such as Softaculous or Fantastico. The auto installer script varies by web hosting providers. WordPress is known for its "Famous 5-Minute Installation" that is documented on the WordPress Codex.[8] If a development environment needs to be set up where certain features can be tested before implementing them on a live website, this version can be used for that.

Figure 3-5.   *WordPress is available for download from* `www.wordpress.org`

---

[7]`https://wordpress.org/about/requirements/`
[8]`https://codex.wordpress.org/Installing_WordPress#Famous_5-Minute_Installation`

The main difference between wordpress.org and wordpress.com is that wordpress. com handles everything for you for a fee whereas wordpress.org does not. When you visit www.wordpress.com, you can sign up for one of four account types:

- Free

- Personal

- Premium

- Business

Many people choose the free option because once the account is created, they can immediately start blogging or creating a website. There is no better example of the saying, "Everything that is free isn't good and everything that is good is not free" than this for many reasons. First, your domain name will contain wordpress.com (i.e., yourwebsite123.wordpress.com) and will not allow a unique domain name until upgraded to one of the other options. Depending on your needs, this could be problematic because your target audience probably won't remember a long domain name. For creating an online store, it would be best to purchase your own unique domain name from a domain registrar service such as Network Solutions, Namecheap, or through a web hosting provider who sometimes offers free domain names when signing up for web hosting. Another benefit of having a custom domain name is it presents a professional image and brand for a business and a website. First impressions are a lasting impression, and this is crucial for an online store.

With the WordPress.com free account, many features such as plugins, themes, and source code modification are limited, so you won't experience the full power of WordPress until you upgrade to another account. Plugins cannot be installed. You will also be subjected to ads and limited storage. If you are uncertain as to which account you should use, you can always choose the Compare Plans option (Figure 3-6) to review the differences.

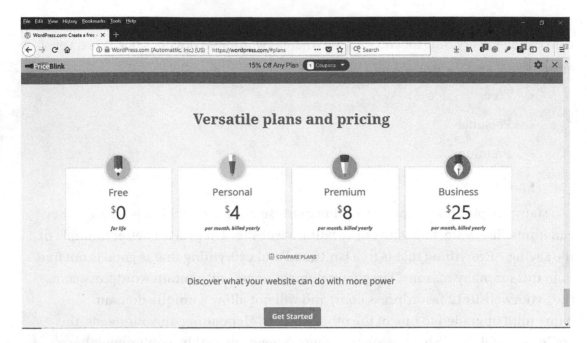

Figure 3-6. *WordPress Plans and Pricing from* www.wordpresss.com

WordPress Requirements

While you are probably going to use an external web hosting company for your online store, there are some that might want to host their online store themselves. Nevertheless, it is a good idea to know the WordPress requirements so that you can compare them when choosing web hosting. Compared to other applications, its requirements are simple. According to WordPress.org,[9] the recommended requirements necessary to run WordPress are:

- PHP version 7.2 or greater.

- MySQL version 5.6 or greater or MariaDB version 10.0 or greater.

- HTTPS support.

The only other thing that you will need is a computer or mobile device to log in to the WordPress administration panel to work on your website or blog.

---

[9]https://wordpress.org/about/requirements/

Installing WordPress on a Web Host

Once you purchase web hosting, the web host will provide login credentials to access the cPanel. The cPanel allows remote access to install software on the web host's web server via a one-click auto script installer. Some of the popular auto script installers are MOJO Marketplace, Fantastico, Softaculous, and Quickinstall. These installation instructions are based on the Bluehost web host who uses MOJO Marketplace.

Once in the cPanel, click on Install WordPress in the Website Section (Figure 3-7).

Figure 3-7. *Installing WordPress from web host cPanel*

Select the domain name from the domain drop-down menu along with the installation directory (Figure 3-8).

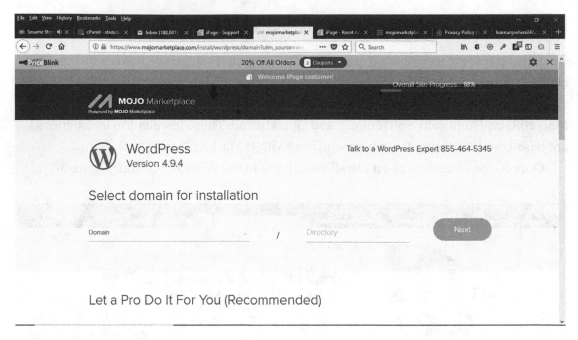

Figure 3-8. *Selecting a domain name for installation during WordPress installation*

On the Administration Screen, change the Site Name, Admin user name, Admin email, and password (Figure 3-9). For added security, do not use Admin as the Admin user name. Hackers know that most WordPress users might use this username, which makes it easier to hack a site. Instead choose another Admin name that is more difficult for hackers to guess. Likewise, for the password, do not use Password because it is easy to guess as well. It is a good practice to choose a password that is 8–10 alphanumeric characters with a combination of upper and lowercase letters and special characters. Make sure that all checkboxes are checked. Click the Next button.

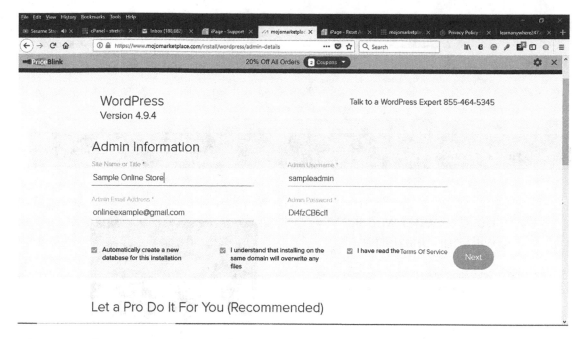

Figure 3-9. *Creating Admin Information during WordPress installation*

A progress bar in the top right of the screen shows the percentage completion of the installation. Once the WordPress installation is complete, a confirmation will be displayed (Figure 3-10). A link is also provided to view login information. The next step would be to select a theme. Since the website will be an e-commerce site using WooCommerce, the Storefront theme will be selected in Chapter 5.

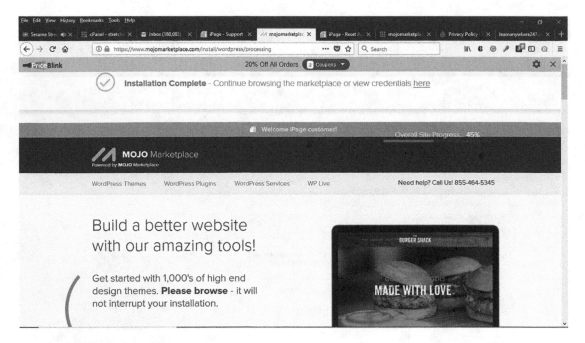

Figure 3-10. *Installation Complete message that appears means WordPress has been successfully installed*

Post-Installation Setup

Now that WordPress has been successfully installed, some items need to be addressed to help clean up the installation and secure it. In its current installation state, WordPress is using system-generated defaults except for the provided administration information. Before launching a site, the following items should be addressed.

Delete sample posts, pages, images, and comments. Items created during the installation that will not be used consume disk space. If their visibility is set to Public along with a Published Status, they will appear on a website. It is a good practice to delete any sample posts, pages, images, and comments that do not belong to a project. For example, WordPress creates a Sample page during installation that should be deleted. To see all pages, click Pages ➤ All Pages (Figure 3-11). Once all pages that need to be deleted have been identified, click the checkbox beside their title and select Move To Trash from the Bulk Actions drop-down. Click the Apply button.

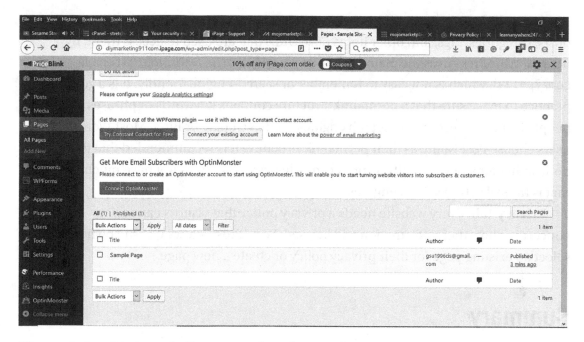

Figure 3-11. *Listing of all pages within the WordPress Dashboard*

Delete Unused Plugins and Themes. WordPress installs default plugins such as Hello Dolly, which displays the song lyrics to the song "Hello Dolly." It does not serve a purpose and will not be used. Likewise, themes such as Twenty Seventeen, Twenty Fifteen, and Twenty Sixteen are installed to help customize a project. Once a theme is activated, it is a good practice to delete the unused themes because they can slow down the performance of a site as well as consume space.

Settings. In the WordPress Dashboard, there are settings that need to be reviewed for correctness. Here are some settings to review on the various tabs.

General Tab. The General Tab contains general information pertaining to the WordPress project. The Tagline should be changed from "Just another WordPress site" to a short, descriptive statement about the company. To make sure that unauthorized users cannot obtain membership to a website, it is a good practice to make sure the anyone can register checkbox is unchecked and the new user default role is Subscriber. Likewise, it is good to set the Time Zone along with the Start of the Week.

Permalinks Tab. Permalinks are how WordPress structures its URL's. All pages, posts, categories, tags, and other items have URLs that are used to access them. By default, WordPress uses the plain option for permalinks (i.e., `www.yoursitename.com/?p=123`), which is not easy to remember or search-engine friendly. It is a good practice to make sure that a permalink structure contains keywords or phrases to help people locate the resource in search engines such as Google or Bing. Most WordPress users choose Post Name as their permalink structure. It is recommended that this is done either for a new WordPress project or when a project does not have much content that is ranked within search engines.

Privacy Tab. Every website needs a privacy policy that visitors can review concerning how their information will be used. WordPress allows website owners to select an existing page for their privacy policy or create a new page.

Summary

WordPress provides scalability and flexibility for any size business wanting to establish a web presence. With its ease of installation and use, it helps make creating a blog, website, or online store less intimidating and cost effective. In the next chapter, WooCommerce and its e-commerce features will be explored to show how to create an online store.

CHAPTER 4

WooCommerce for E-commerce

What is the simplest way to accept credit and debit cards online?

Entering this phrase in Google will return over two million search results. Those are a lot of results to narrow down. However, no matter how many results there are, one thing remains the same: it all depends on an organization's estimated volume of transactions and comfort and experience level with e-commerce terms such as merchant account, payment gateway, and others. Unfortunately, many are not familiar with these terms nor have the time or resources to understand or adequately implement them. As a result, they cannot accept online payments through their websites and miss out on the opportunity to grow their businesses locally and globally along with potential sales. With all the online payment options available, one option remains a top favorite: PayPal.

PayPal Overview

With all the emerging technology in mobile banking and mobile commerce, many entrepreneurs, small- to medium-sized businesses, and consumers continue to use PayPal to receive and send money online. Brick and mortar stores such as Dollar General offer PayPal to customers as a payment option at checkout.

What is so special about PayPal? It is available to both consumers and businesses. PayPal allows consumers to create a free account and then add a credit card or checking account to their account that can be used when making purchases or sending or receiving money online by logging into their account on any device or through the PayPal app. With the increased number of data breaches of consumer information, this is one step that many consumers take to protect their credit card information. Although nothing is 100 percent secure, it is a small step in the right direction. In other words,

© Lisa Sims 2018
L. Sims, *Building Your Online Store With WordPress and WooCommerce*,
https://doi.org/10.1007/978-1-4842-3846-2_4

doing something is better than doing nothing. PayPal and other payment gateways such as Stripe must adhere to a set of security standards to protect consumers' payment information. These standards are implemented by the Payment Card Industry Data Security Standards (PCI DSS) known as PCI Compliance. Even using PayPal, businesses still need to know and understand what it means to be PCI Compliant. To become more familiar with PCI compliance, visit *www.pcicomplianceguide.org*.

Businesses of all sizes can also set up PayPal accounts but are charged a fixed fee and percentage (varies between U.S. and International) of each transaction to accept credit cards online. It also offers encryption to protect transaction information. What makes PayPal so appealing? According to the PayPal website, over 203 million shoppers use PayPal to check out online.[1] Here are some other interesting PayPal statistics about online shoppers:[2]

- 32 percent of millennials use PayPal.

- 25 percent of millennials prefer PayPal for paying for and receiving money. Among that group, 42 percent prefer using PayPal on their smartphones.

Founded in December 1998 as Confinity and acquired by eBay in 2002, PayPal has become one of the online payment method leaders. How big of an industry leader are they? According to a 2014 Techworld.com article, as many as four billion payments were processed through PayPal's e-commerce system.[3] Why is this? PayPal has brand recognition among consumers, which also establishes credibility for those businesses who offer PayPal as a payment method. It is also a trusted e-commerce brand that most business and consumers have used to sell or purchase items online, send money, or send electronic invoices for products or services. Whether as a buyer or seller, PayPal provides convenience to send and receive money online and from any mobile device as well as from the app. Chapter 7 will discuss more about PayPal's and other payment gateway's roles in a business-to-consumer (B2C) or business-to-business (B2B) transaction when creating an online store.

---

[1]https://www.paypal.com/us/webapps/mpp/accept-payments-online

[2]https://www.digitaldoughnut.com/articles/2016/april/the-most-preferred-payments-paypal-joins-the-big

[3]https://www.techworld.com/picture-gallery/business/history-of-paypal-1998-now-3630386/

Compared to some of its competitors, PayPal offers an all-in-one solution with no setup fee, monthly fee (depending on plan), or termination fee along with credit card processing fees for businesses based on total sales volume. With PayPal, micropayments (transactions of $10 or less) are charged higher percentages (varies between U.S. and International) plus a fixed fee. No merchant account or payment gateway is needed. PayPal handles everything. However, there are charges for other online merchant services such as chargebacks, refunds, and others that are listed on PayPal's website. Entrepreneurs and small businesses can benefit from PayPal's services and quickly accept credit cards as opposed to securing an Internet merchant account through a banking institution, which can be time consuming and expensive. However, PayPal is not the only payment gateway that can be used, but it is trusted by many consumers.

What is an Internet merchant account? First, let's define a merchant account. A merchant account is a bank account where money is first deposited when a consumer makes an online purchase before being deposited into a business's bank account. An Internet merchant account is "a merchant account specifically designed to hold the proceeds from the online payment processing of credit cards."[4] In a brick and mortar business, a merchant account would be needed for each accepted credit card type. This is not the case for online stores. One notable difference between a merchant and Internet merchant account is the fees. Fees are typically higher with Internet merchant accounts due to the perceived risk involved with dealing with businesses that process small sales volumes. If PayPal is not used, a payment gateway would be required to authenticate and authorize or decline the online credit card transactions, which can be expensive. To compare online payment gateway prices, visit `www.formstack.com/payment-gateway-comparison`.

When most entrepreneurs or brick and mortar small businesses want to sell products or services online from their website, they typically start with PayPal because it is inexpensive, quick, and easy to add PayPal's "Buy Now" buttons to their website. Adding PayPal's "Buy Now" buttons on a website works well to sell a few items when inventory is limited or when consumers are only interested in purchasing one item during a visit. However, as more inventory items are added or changed, "Buy Now" buttons might need to be replaced with a more scalable solution such as a shopping cart. A virtual shopping cart is like a physical grocery cart in which customers fill their cart with multiple items before heading to checkout. PayPal does offer a shopping cart solution where "Buy Now" buttons would be replaced with "Add To Cart" buttons.

---

[4]`https://www.thebalancesmb.com/merchant-account-2948421`

Googling the phrase "e-commerce solutions" returns over eight million results, which again makes it difficult to quickly narrow down and select the right one for a business's needs. Popular e-commerce solutions such as Shopify with over 600,000 business shops make it simple to sell products online and on social media sites such as Facebook. Another option is Facebook Shops. Facebook Shops allows businesses to set up online stores to sell products and services to potential Facebook customers. With all these and other options available, it is important to realize that there is no perfect e-commerce solution. The solution that you choose should focus on a positive return on investment (ROI)), low total cost of ownership, easy setup and use, and scalability as your business and needs grow. Since there are so many options available, why choose WooCommerce?

What Is WooCommerce?

Although many might not be as familiar with WooCommerce as some of the other popular e-commerce solutions such as PayPal or Shopify, it is still just as popular. WooCommerce is an open source e-commerce platform used with WordPress self-hosted websites to create online stores (Figure 4-1). It is a comprehensive, do-it-yourself e-commerce solution that is installed as a WordPress plugin. Once installed, it is available from within the WordPress Dashboard, which makes it straightforward to manage and update. It uses the simple but professional looking Storefront theme to create an online store's appearance and layout. Recall from Chapter 3 that themes are the outward appearance of a website that visitors see. The Storefront theme is the default WooCommerce online store theme. However, it can be customized through its Storefront Extensions Bundle that at the time of this writing costs $69. Likewise, WooCommerce Storefront Child themes are available for purchase from the WooCommerce website.

According to Builtwith.com, there were over two million WooCommerce websites online, and most of those are business related at the time of this writing.[5] Other business categories that use WooCommerce include shopping, entertainment, health, technology, social, and education. Compared to its Shopify competitor which has 0.2 percent of the e-commerce platform market share, WooCommerce accounts for 0.6 percent with most of the businesses residing in the United States and the United Kingdom. At the time of this writing, WooCommerce has been downloaded over 43 million times and continues to increase daily.[6]

---

[5]https://trends.builtwith.com/shop/WooCommerce
[6]https://woocommerce.com/

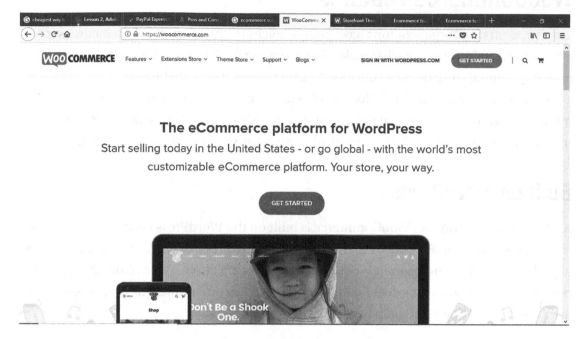

Figure 4-1. *WooCommerce website homepage*

WooCommerce is used by startups as well as established businesses. Some of the businesses that use WooCommerce include:

- Weber

- Singer

- Ripley's Believe It or Not

- Mikasa Sports USA

- Printing New York

- Native

- Alder Creek

- Ghost Bed

- World Vision

- Fusion Jerky

- Miss Jones Baking Company

WooCommerce Features

Entrepreneurs and organizations have many choices to choose from when it comes to e-commerce solutions, but what makes WooCommerce different? What features does it offer to potential store owners considering using it over its competitors?

Once downloaded and installed, WooCommerce provides online store owners with many core features for free that can be used to quickly and efficiently set up and launch their initial online store. What are some of these features? Let's look at some of these.

Built on WordPress

As previously mentioned, WooCommerce is built on the WordPress content management system. For those experienced with WordPress, they can capitalize on their experience while reducing their WooCommerce learning curve. What about WordPress novices? Since WordPress's dashboard is intuitive to use and numerous online resources are available, they can find help to get up to speed quickly.

No Upfront or Monthly Cost

Since the WooCommerce plugin is open source software, it requires no setup cost or monthly usage charge. However, WooCommerce themes and extensions involve a cost. With most startups and small businesses having limited budgets and resources, WooCommerce can be a good e-commerce choice

30-Day Money Back Guarantee

Choosing an e-commerce solution for businesses big or small is a big decision. Once an e-commerce solution is chosen and implemented, it is natural to experience buyer's remorse at some point. On its website, WooCommerce offers a 30-day money back guarantee and refund policy that can be submitted through their website.

Safe and Secured Payments for Customers

Cyber security is a hot topic these days along with identity theft and data breaches. When consumers shop in brick and mortar or click and mortar stores, they worry about whether their credit card and personal information is being properly secured and protected. With so many data breaches being frequently reported in the news, consumers are concerned and cautious when making credit card purchases. WooCommerce provides security features to help businesses secure and protect consumers' credit card information.

Sell Physical or Digital Products

Not sure whether to sell physical or digital products? No problem! WooCommerce allows store owners to easily sell anything physical or digital within the same store. They can even sell a combination of both. Store owners can even create and sell online classes using the Sensei extension.

Multiple Payment Gateways

PayPal is the default payment gateway prepackaged with WooCommerce for accepting and processing credit cards and PayPal account payments. Want to use a payment gateway other than PayPal? No problem! Other payment gateways that are available as WooCommerce extensions include:

- Amazon Payments

- Stripe

- Authorize.net

- PayFast

- FirstData

- PayPal Express

WooCommerce also makes accepting BACS (Bankers Automated Clearing Service) and cash on delivery payments. It also allows international transactions, which allows store owners to take their online business globally.

Unlimited Inventory

Starting out, store owners might have a limited number of items to sell but increase them over time. Store owners do not have to worry about reaching a product limit within

WooCommerce. There is no limit to the number of items that can be sold. Store owners are only limited by their available inventory.

Global Support

The WooCommerce website offers various types of support resources to help answer any questions that might arise while creating an online store. What types of support are available? Online support consists of:

- WooCommerce documentation

- Online help desk

- Video

- Idea Board/Forum

- Blog tutorials

- Developer blog

Extend WooCommerce with Extensions

Once a WooCommerce store is created and launched, it is never finished. There will always be opportunities to improve sales, customers' shopping experiences, and more just like in traditional brick and mortar stores. With WooCommerce's numerous free and paid extensions (also called plugins), store owners can extend their store's core features and functions for free or for a fee at any time. Recall from Chapter 3 that plugins are "ways to extend and add to the functionality that already exists in WordPress."[7] According to the WooCommerce website, there are over 400 extensions available in various categories. These extensions are available from the WooCommerce website and consist of:

- Email marketing

- Shipping management

- Subscription management

- Store management

---

[7]https://codex.wordpress.org/Plugins

- Enhancements

- Product Add-ons

- Discounts and coupons

- And more

Extensions are also available for free or for a fee for the WooCommerce Storefront theme. These extensions make it possible to customize the theme without requiring any technical or web design expertise. Some of these extensions include:

- Storefront product sharing

- Storefront product pagination

- Storefront reviews

- Storefront pricing tables

- And more

iOS Mobile Device Store Management

Would it not be nice to manage an online store from a mobile device? Since most entrepreneurs and business owners are multitaskers and always have their smartphones or mobile devices nearby, they can manage their online stores at their fingertips. With the iOS WooCommerce app, store owners have the freedom and flexibility to manage their stores from any iOS mobile device such as an iPhone or iPad anytime and from anywhere. Store owners can view sales reports, add products, and other store management tasks without the hassle of being in front of a laptop or computer or taking along a laptop. Talk about having a mobile store in your pocket (or purse).

E-commerce on Any Page

Entrepreneurs and small business owners can sell anything from any page of their website. How? Since WooCommerce is built upon WordPress, it takes advantage of WordPress's shortcodes. What is a shortcode? WordPress.com defines a shortcode as "a WordPress-specific code that lets you do nifty things with very little effort. Shortcodes can embed files or create objects that would normally require lots of complicated, ugly code in just one line."[8] WooCommerce provides the flexibility to not only create an e-commerce website but also sell anything via shortcodes on a blog post. How cool is that?

Meetups

Social media platforms such as Facebook, Periscope, and Instagram make virtual meetups convenient and effortless to attend, but occasionally it is also good to attend in-person meetups. These meetups help entrepreneurs expand their network and develop potential business relationships with like-minded people. WooCommerce hosts in-person meetups worldwide for WooCommerce enthusiasts to network, collaborate, and discover new features and functions for their online stores. These meetups can be located using meetup.com or the meetup.com app or the WooCommerce website. Interested enthusiasts can even sign up to host their own WooCommerce meetups in their area. What better way to learn more about WooCommerce than to teach others how to use it? All the information concerning how to host a meetup is available on woocommerce.com.

Other WooCommerce Products

As a business grows, so does its needs. If it does not keep trying, it will eventually end up dying. Solutions such as WooCommerce are scalable enough to grow with an organization's current and future needs. WooCommerce offers other products that can extend an online store's functionality. Some of these products are:

- Storefront – the default WooCommerce theme

- Sensei – WordPress learning management system plugin for creating online coursework

- Sensei Extension - WordPress plugins to enhance the Sensei classroom

- Other Plugins – WordPress plugins that can help create a better experience for users as well as store owners

---

[8]https://en.support.wordpress.com/shortcodes/

For those businesses looking for an e-commerce solution, WooCommerce is an excellent choice with many benefits and features to quickly set up an online store.

Installing WooCommerce

Before installing WooCommerce, adding inventory, and launching a store to the Web, certain steps should be followed. For starters, securing a domain name for an online store is crucial for several reasons. First, potential customers will use this to locate an online store. Even if they do not know a company's website address, they can still use search engines such as Google to find it. When choosing a domain name, keep it short and easy for potential customers to remember. It might be tempting to create a long, descriptive URL, but if no one can remember it or how to spell it, it is useless. Having a memorable domain name also ties into a company's brand.

Once a domain name has been chosen, where should it be registered? Some people prefer to register their domain separately and use companies such as `www.namecheap.com`, `www.godaddy.com`, `www.networksolutions.com`, and others to do it. Most web hosting companies will also register a new domain name or transfer an existing domain name during the web hosting sign-up process. If you are uncertain about who to select for web hosting, it is recommended to consider using managed WordPress hosting. Managed WordPress hosting is hosting that handles all aspects of running and maintaining WordPress. Unlike shared hosting, it can be more expensive, but it provides faster performance because it is optimized for WordPress websites. A few popular managed WordPress hosts include WPEngine.com, Siteground.com, `Bluehost.com`, and FlyWheel.[9] Many managed hosts offer WooCommerce and WooCommerce plans. Likewise, `www.woocommerce.com` also recommends hosting solutions under the We Recommend Section at the bottom of their homepage.

Once web hosting is obtained, it is now time to install WooCommerce. WooCommerce can be installed by either FTP or directly through a web host's cPanel. Let's look at installing WooCommerce via FTP.

---

[9]`https://www.wpkube.com/best-managed-wordpress-hosting/`

Installing WooCommerce via FTP

The WooCommerce plugin can be downloaded from the WordPress.org Plugins directory. After search for WooCommerce on the Plugins page, the WooCommerce plugin page is displayed with its information along with a download button (Figure 4-2).

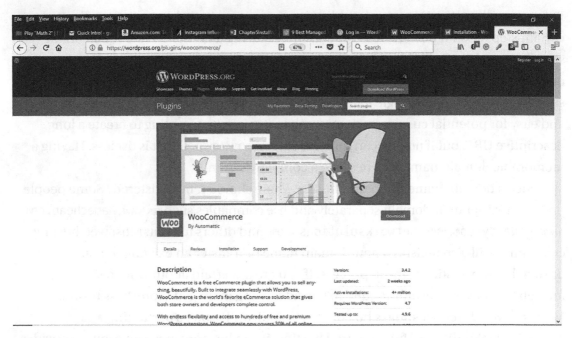

Figure 4-2. *WooCommerce plugin available for download from Wordpress.org*

To FTP the WooCommerce plugin to a web server, click the download button and save the zip file to a location on the computer (Figure 4-3). Once downloaded, the file can either be unzipped or not. The zipped file can be uploaded to the Plugins menu via the WordPress Dashboard (Figure 4-4). It can also be unzipped and installed via an FTP program. An FTP program allows a file stored on one computer to be transferred to another computer's location via an Internet FTP connection. Web hosts provide an FTP URL, FTP username, and password for a domain once hosting has been purchased. This information is used to connect to the web server. Using an FTP program or the web host's control panel, upload the folder to the WordPress installation wp-content/plugins directory (Figure 4-5). The plugin can now be activated from the Plugins menu in the WordPress Dashboard (Figure 4-4).

Figure 4-3. *Saving WooCommerce plugin to a computer*

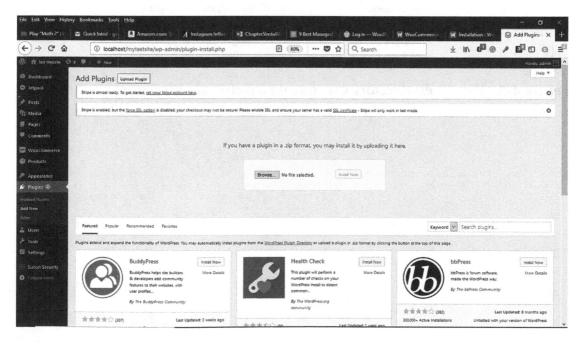

Figure 4-4. *Uploading a zipped plugin in the WordPress Dashboard*

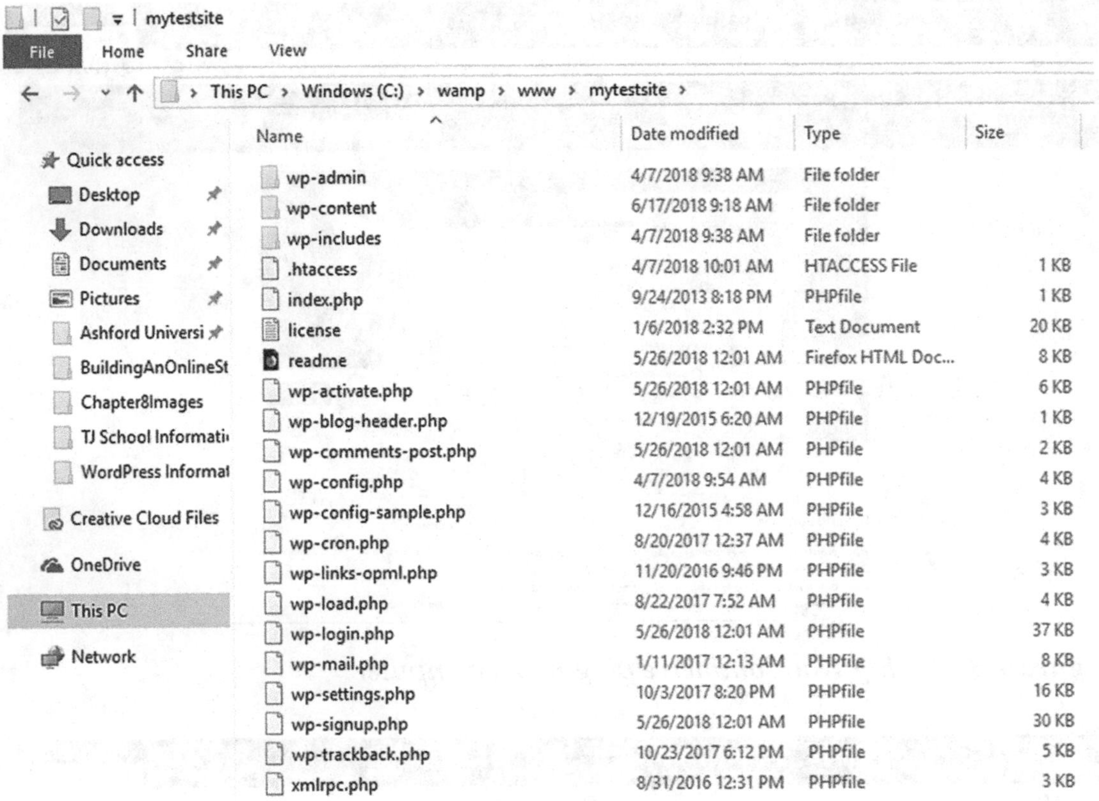
mytestsite
File
Home
Share
View
This PC › Windows (C:) › wamp › www › mytestsite ›
Name
Date modified
Type
Size
Quick access
Desktop
Downloads
Documents
Pictures
Ashford Universi
BuildingAnOnlineSt
Chapter8Images
TJ School Informati
WordPress Informat
Creative Cloud Files
OneDrive
This PC
Network
wp-admin 4/7/2018 9:38 AM File folder
wp-content 6/17/2018 9:18 AM File folder
wp-includes 4/7/2018 9:38 AM File folder
.htaccess 4/7/2018 10:01 AM HTACCESS File 1 KB
index.php 9/24/2013 8:18 PM PHPfile 1 KB
license 1/6/2018 2:32 PM Text Document 20 KB
readme 5/26/2018 12:01 AM Firefox HTML Doc... 8 KB
wp-activate.php 5/26/2018 12:01 AM PHPfile 6 KB
wp-blog-header.php 12/19/2015 6:20 AM PHPfile 1 KB
wp-comments-post.php 5/26/2018 12:01 AM PHPfile 2 KB
wp-config.php 4/7/2018 9:54 AM PHPfile 4 KB
wp-config-sample.php 12/16/2015 4:58 AM PHPfile 3 KB
wp-cron.php 8/20/2017 12:37 AM PHPfile 4 KB
wp-links-opml.php 11/20/2016 9:46 PM PHPfile 3 KB
wp-load.php 8/22/2017 7:52 AM PHPfile 4 KB
wp-login.php 5/26/2018 12:01 AM PHPfile 37 KB
wp-mail.php 1/11/2017 12:13 AM PHPfile 8 KB
wp-settings.php 10/3/2017 8:20 PM PHPfile 16 KB
wp-signup.php 5/26/2018 12:01 AM PHPfile 30 KB
wp-trackback.php 10/23/2017 6:12 PM PHPfile 5 KB
xmlrpc.php 8/31/2016 12:31 PM PHPfile 3 KB

***Figure 4-5.** WordPress directory structure on a web host web server*

WooCommerce can also be installed through the WordPress Dashboard. Once logged into your web host's WordPress Dashboard with your credentials, locate the Plugins menu and click Add New (Figure 4-6).

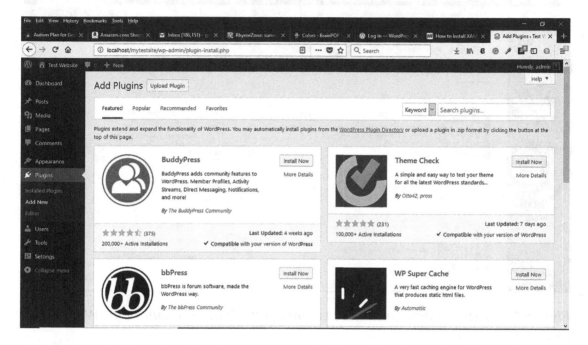

Figure 4-6. *Adding the WooCommerce plugin from WordPress Dashboard*

In the search plugins box, type in WooCommerce and hit enter. Once the WooCommerce plugin is returned, click the Install Now button (Figure 4-7).

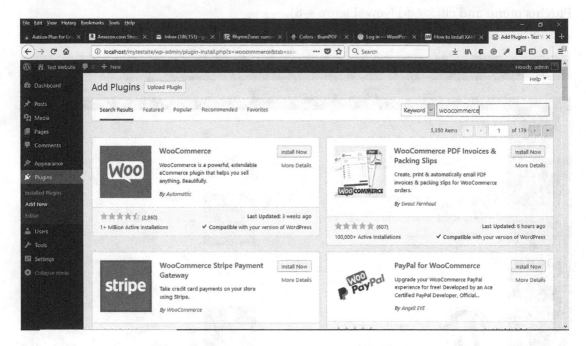

Figure 4-7. *Adding WooCommerce plugin via the Plugins menu in the WordPress Dashboard*

Once the WooCommerce installation is complete, an activate button will appear. The activate button will launch a setup wizard to continue configuring your store's initial settings (Figure 4-8). Before setting up your online store, let's look at e-commerce themes and their roles in WooCommerce. Chapter 5 will address e-commerce themes.

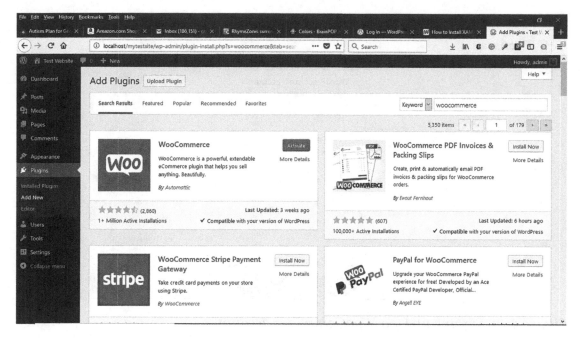

Figure 4-8. *Activating WooCommerce after installing it in the WordPress Dashboard*

To get started, visit `www.woocommerce.com` and click the Get Started button on the homepage (Figure 4-1). To create a WooCommerce account to manage purchases, support tickets, and subscriptions, WooCommerce requires either an existing WordPress.com account, create a new WordPress.com account, or continue with Google (Figure 4-9). Recall from Chapter 3 that wordpress.com is a hosted account.

Figure 4-9. Signing up for a WooCommerce account

Summary

WooCommerce offers many features that can help small- and medium-sized businesses create a scalable online store for physical or digital products. With its intuitive installation via FTP or within the WordPress Dashboard, WooCommerce can be quickly installed. In the next chapter, WooCommerce's configuration settings for creating an online store will be explored.

CHAPTER 5

E-commerce Themes

Before adding any products to an online store powered by WordPress and WooCommerce, WooCommerce must first be installed. Chapter 4 provided an illustrated overview of the WooCommerce installation process. Now that WooCommerce is installed, what's next? The next step is to think about the online store's first impression to potential customers.

Where do you begin to create a good first impression for potential customers? Depending on who you ask, you could receive many different answers. However, for an online store, the first place to focus on providing potential customers a positive first impression is with the storefront or homepage. What is a storefront? It's the first thing that a potential customer sees before entering a store. For online stores, a storefront equates to an e-commerce theme.

Enhancing the Customer Experience

Prior to a new brick and mortar store opening its doors to the public for business, the customer experience for potential customers has already been discussed and planned. By carefully considering customers' experiences ahead of time, a new brick and mortar store can brainstorm various techniques and methods to encourage customers to not only visit the store but also make in-store purchases and become repeat shoppers. Why is this important? Shelley Kohan, vice president of retail consulting at in-store analytics company RetailNext, provided some insight into the customer experience in a *Chain Store Age* column. She shared that "providing the 'In-Store Experience' is vital for physical stores to win over foot traffic and brand loyalty. Shoppers want to explore, learn and have fun. Above all else, they want that instant gratification from products that are in stock and easy to find."[1]

---

[1] https://compassmag.3ds.com/3/Industry/BRICKS-MORTAR-Creating-stores-that-consumers-want-to-visit

© Lisa Sims 2018
L. Sims, *Building Your Online Store With WordPress and WooCommerce*,
https://doi.org/10.1007/978-1-4842-3846-2_5

With brick and mortar stores, the customer experience involves several components such as:

- Lighting

- Music

- Product displays

- Signage

- Décor

- Color selection

- Product selection

- Storefront entrance

- Customer service

- Complimentary gifts

Lighting

When shoppers visit a brick and mortar store, they expect good lighting to clearly see the products and their details. For an online store, it is impossible to duplicate the same physical lighting structures, but there are a few things that can be done to help shoppers. For instance, making sure that product or service images use light-colored solid backgrounds that make it easy for shoppers to see the details will help them during their shopping experience. Also, using good lighting when taking pictures can also help produce good product and service images.

Music

Providing music during a brick and mortar shopping experience has many benefits. Most brick and mortar stores play some type of background music to help enhance shoppers' experiences. According to The State of Brick & Mortar 2017 research, 84 percent of U.S. shoppers said music makes the shopping experience more enjoyable.[2]

---

[2]https://smallbiztrends.com/2017/09/effects-of-music-on-shoppers.html

Some stores select their music selections to help influence shoppers' moods and match the store's brand or image. These stores have paid for some type of music subscription that will allow them to use the music.

For online stores, using music is more complicated because it involves the issue of copyright. Using someone else's music without permission or consent that is not royalty free violates copyright laws. Also, some shoppers find music playing on websites distracting and annoying. It is a best practice to not include music on a website. If it is included, it should have a specific purpose and have a royalty-free license. What does royalty-free music mean? Premiumbeat.com defines royalty-free music as "a type of music licensing that allows the purchaser to pay for the music license only once and to use the music for as long as desired."[3] There is still a cost involved in purchasing the music, but it can be used numerous times and on numerous places. Lastly, shoppers should have the ability to turn the music on or off as needed.

Product Displays

Brick and mortar product displays can entice reluctant shoppers to buy. Creative product displays can also help persuade shoppers to make a purchase. Think about some of the Super Bowl product displays at stores such as Walmart and Target. Did they not influence shoppers to buy them? Duplicating this type of product display in an online store will take some creative thinking but it can be done (Figure 5-1).

---

[3]https://www.premiumbeat.com/blog/what-is-royalty-free-music/

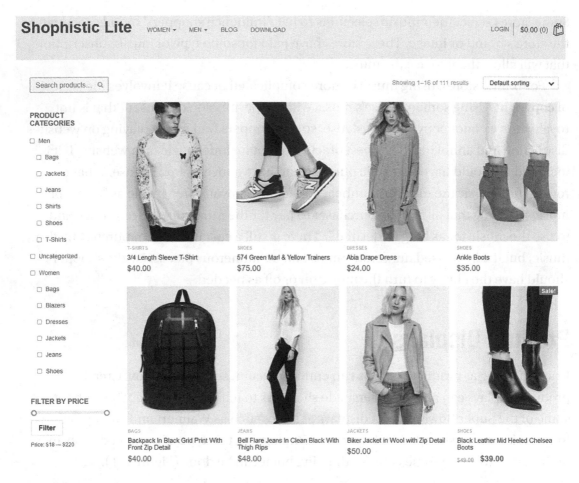

Figure 5-1. *Shophistic Lite theme that demonstrates product displays and categories*

Signs

When shopping in-store, shoppers have been conditioned to look for various signs to help locate products along with potential sale items. Whether the signs are located at the end or above aisles or on product displays, shoppers depend on these during their shopping excursion. For example, Walmart uses the Rollback signs to indicate that a product's price has been lowered.

Online stores can implement similar signs to help shoppers during their shopping quickly locate what they need. One way to accomplish this is by using descriptive categories for products (or services). Providing shoppers with the ability to search for products (or services) is another way to help shoppers quickly locate what they need without relying on signs.

Décor

Trying to duplicate brick and mortar décor is impossible for online stores. It is also one of the reasons that many store owners decide to open an online store. Choosing an e-commerce theme that has an attractive and simple-to-use design can help provide shoppers with a similar online décor.

Color Selection

After choosing an e-commerce theme, it is a good practice to select a color palette that closely matches a store's brand and image. Selecting complementary colors will not only help make online stores more appealing to shoppers but can also help influence shoppers' moods in a similar manner as music in brick and mortar stores.

Product Selection

Determining what products to sell is another challenge not only with brick and mortar stores but also e-commerce stores. Choosing the right mix of products and displaying them in a logical order will help shoppers make their selections.

Storefront Entrance

In the same manner that brick and mortar storefront entrances are attractive and appealing, an online storefront entrance should be the same. The e-commerce theme's storefront layout should be clean and invite shoppers to click through the store (Figure 5-2).

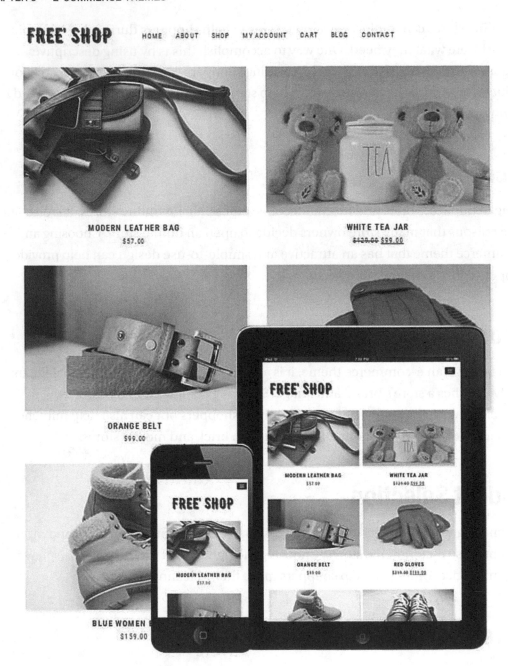

Figure 5-2. *Free Shop WooCommerce theme*

Customer Service

Oftentimes, shoppers might have questions about products (or services) or need to return or exchange an item. These tasks are typically handled by customer service. In an online store, shoppers should be able to easily locate customer service contacts or possibly begin an online chat with an online representative.

Complimentary Gifts

Most shoppers enjoy free gifts. Many brick and mortar stores conduct occasional sampling events within the store where shoppers can either sample free food or receive free gifts from watching a demonstration. Offering a complimentary gift with or without purchase can encourage shoppers to visit an online store.

Typically, these components are handled by a team of people with various titles and roles. Regardless of their titles and roles, they are all working together to achieve the same goal: a positive and repeatable customer experience that results in sales. How does this relate to online stores?

Even though ordering online is convenient and sometimes cheaper than brick and mortar stores, online retailers must try harder to re-create certain aspects of the in-store customer experience online. For online stores, the customer experience begins the moment potential customers type in a company's URL into their web browser and land on a company's homepage. A company's homepage is the equivalent of a brick and mortar's storefront entrance. It is the first (and possibly last) point of contact where the customer experience begins. If it does not look clean, professional, appealing, or inviting, first-time visitors will initially visit but quickly leave and possibly never return. How can this be prevented? Themes can help start the online customer experience on the right foot.

WooCommerce Theme Overview

WooCommerce themes can be found on the WooCommerce website, `www.woocommerce.com`. These themes are compatible with WooCommerce, which will reduce potential technical issues but does not guarantee that they are compatible with plugins and add-ons that are used. WooCommerce's popular theme to use with WooCommerce is the free WordPress theme called Storefront. According to the WooCommerce website, Storefront is "built and maintained by WooCommerce core developers," which means it was designed to work seamlessly with WooCommerce and WooCommerce extensions. It is a popular theme and at the time of this writing has been downloaded over two million times. E-commerce websites that are built using the Storefront theme include:

- Fashion Candi (`www.fashioncandi.com`, see Figure 5-3)

- Inspiring Journals (`www.inspiringjournals.com`, see Figure 5-4)

- Flipbookit (`www.flipbookits.com`)

- Gimme Shoes (`www.gimmeshoes.com`)

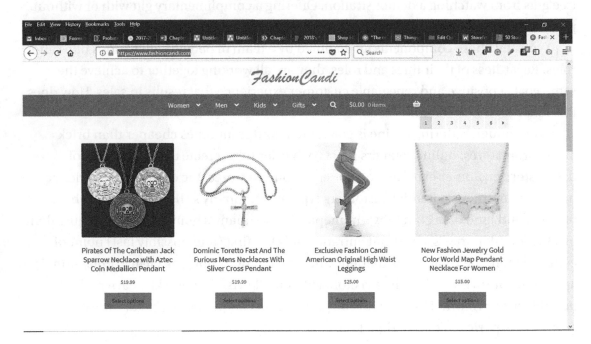

Figure 5-3. *FashionCandi.com e-commerce website using the Storefront Theme*

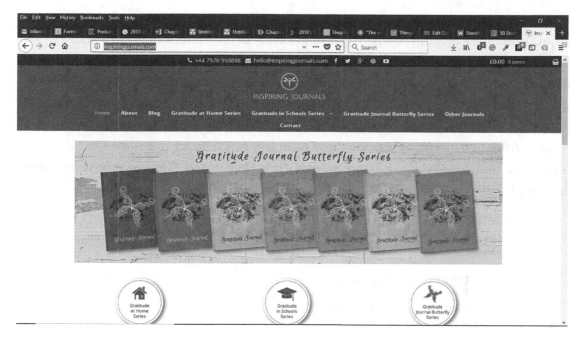

Figure 5-4. *Inspiring Journals (*`www.inspiringjournals.com`*) e-commerce website using the Storefront Theme*

As mentioned in the previous section, "Choosing a Theme," the Storefront Theme offers many of the same features such as:

- Responsive Design

- Accessibility Ready

- E-commerce-focused Homepage

- WooCommerce Integration

- Built from the Underscores starter theme used by Automattic

- Customizable child themes to give your store a new look and feel

- Support available from the WooCommerce support site (`https://docs.woocommerce.com/documentation/themes/storefront`), help desk, and WordPress.org support forums

The Storefront custom shop pages can be modified using the Storefront WooCommerce Customizer, which is now available in the Storefront PowerPack. According to the WooCommerce Docs website, Storefront Powerpack is a combination of the previously offered WooCommerce Designer, Storefront Designer, and Storefront Checkout Customizer extensions, plus brand-new functionality and features.[4] If the Storefront theme's core features are not enough, Storefront extensions are available ranging from free to a fee to provide those extra features. These extensions can be purchased individually or as a bundle ranging from free to $69. Some of those extensions consist of:

- · Storefront Homepage Contact Section

- Storefront Footer Bar

- Storefront Product Sharing

- Storefront Product Pagination

- Storefront Reviews

- Storefront Pricing Tables

As we discussed in the beginning of the chapter, every online store will need a makeover at some point to give it a new look and feel. WooCommerce makes it easy to do this with its Storefront Child Themes (Figure 5-5). These themes are available on the WooCommerce website under the Theme Store navigation and cost about $40. WooCommerce organizes the themes by industries to make themes easy to find.

---

[4]https://docs.woocommerce.com/document/storefront-powerpack/

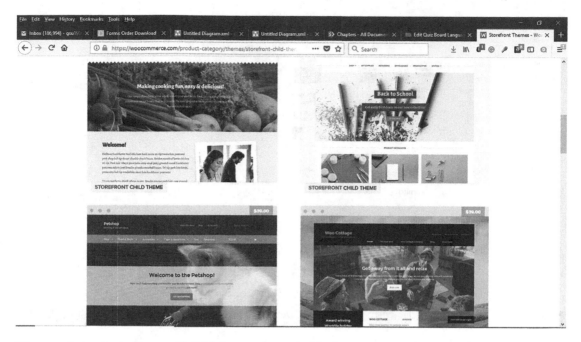

Figure 5-5. *Storefront Child Themes available for purchase on the WooCommerce website*

Besides WooCommerce.com, WooCommerce compatible themes can also be purchased from Themeforest (`https://themeforest.net`) website (Figure 5-6), Templatemonster.com (Figure 5-7), and other online marketplaces. It is a good practice to make sure that the theme is compatible not only with WooCommerce but the particular version of WooCommerce an online store is using (Figure 5-8). It is also good to choose a theme that is well maintained and with good, positive reviews.

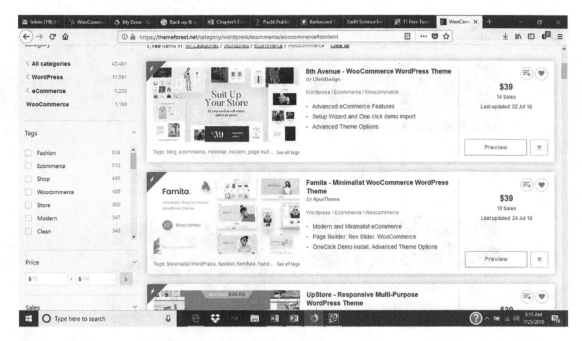

Figure 5-6. *WooCommerce compatible e-commerce themes available for purchase on the Themeforest website*

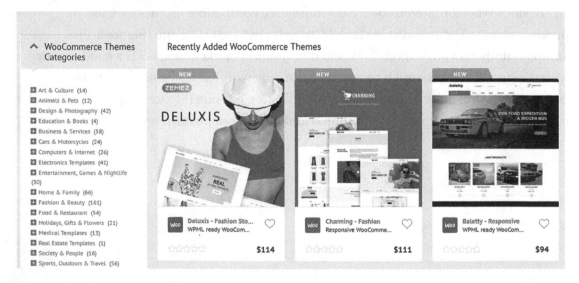

Figure 5-7. *Premium WooCommerce themes from www.templatemonster.com*

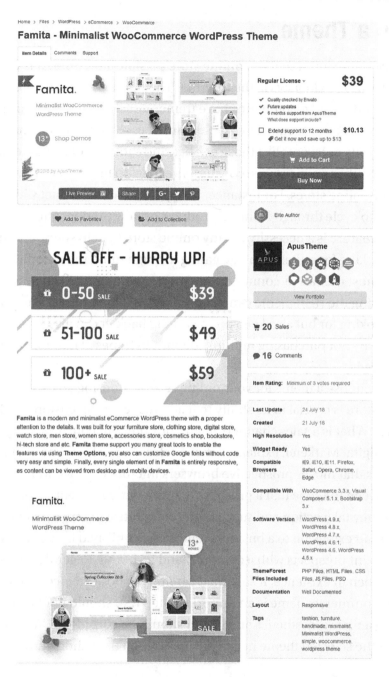

Figure 5-8. *Sample WooCommerce theme from Themeforest.net that shows WooCommerce compatibility information*

Choosing a Theme

An e-commerce theme represents an online store's visible storefront. It is a company's face or brand displayed globally via the Internet. The popularity of the Internet, mobile devices, social media, and e-commerce have tremendously influenced consumers and the way they shop. When consumers visit e-commerce websites, they expect to find attractive storefronts or layouts like those at brick and mortar stores. Based on their past experiences with other online stores, consumers expect to find almost the same set of features at other online stores. For instance, shoppers look for product slider panels that allow them to cycle through featured products or new product offerings. Likewise, having a search feature is a necessity for any online store to help shoppers quickly locate what they are looking for rather than navigating through numerous product or service categories. For most themes (e-commerce and non-e-commerce), a search feature is standard. Choosing the right theme can help prospects and customers not only find what they are looking for but also keep them coming back. It can also save a company time and money by not purchasing multiple themes in hopes of landing the right one that meets its needs.

How do you choose a theme for your online store? Choosing an e-commerce theme for your online store is crucial to its ability to lead prospects and customers through the sales funnel. What is a sales channel? In an Entrepreneur.com article, Ryan Deiss, co-founder of Digital Marketer, explained that a sales channel is a "multi-step, multi-modality process that moves prospective browsers into buyers."[5] He went on to say, "lots must occur between the time that a prospect is aware enough to enter your funnel, to the time when they take action and successfully complete a purchase." An e-commerce theme serves as an extension to a business's already established brand. For startups, it can help acquaint prospects with a company and its brand. Regardless of how long a business has been in existence, it still must carefully choose an e-commerce theme. Choosing an e-commerce theme is an important step that should not be taken lightly. When choosing a theme, aesthetics and layout should be considered but also business goals. How will the selected theme help a business reach their short-term and long-term goals?

What elements should be considered when evaluating a theme? Let's look at a few in the following sections.

---

[5]https://www.entrepreneur.com/article/296526

Easy Installation

Whether you are someone else will create the online store, the theme needs to have an easy setup process. A theme that is difficult and time-consuming to install takes away valuable time and potential money that could be used creating your store.

Responsive and Mobile Ready

Regardless of what device prospects use to access an own online store, the theme should automatically adjust to the device's screen size. As consumers rely more heavily upon their mobile devices, choosing a responsive and mobile-ready theme is no longer an option but a requirement. Without a responsive and mobile-ready theme, many businesses can miss opportunities to convert prospects to customers.

Easily Customizable

Most themes are either free or premium. The problem with some free and fee-based themes is that they can only be customized to a certain point without either requiring a developer or purchasing another theme. Customization can include background colors, font selections, product placement, and more. Themes should be easily customizable to match a business's brand or store theme. The quotation from Heraclitus sums up how change should be viewed: "The only constant in life is change." Once an online store has been operational for a period of time, it might be a good idea to give the store a makeover so that it has a new and fresh look.

AJAX Scripts

What is AJAX? AJAX stands for Asynchronous JavaScript and XML. W3Schools describes AJAX as "allowing web pages to be updated asynchronously by exchanging data with a web server behind the scenes". This means that it is possible to update parts of a web page, without reloading the whole page.[6] W3Schools also provides some other benefits of using AJAX such as:

- Request data from a server – after the page has loaded

- Receive data from a server – after the page has loaded

- Send data to a server – in the background

---

[6]https://www.w3schools.com/xml/ajax_intro.asp

WooCommerce themes that use AJAX scripts provide a richer user experience without waiting for pages to reload.

Load Time

Let's face it. Everyone hates to wait. Besides the limited product selection, long lines at brick and mortar stores are one reason many people switched to online shopping or mobile ordering. Once people find your online store, the last thing they want to do is wait for the theme and its pages to load. People are impatient and have short attention spans and want instant gratification. To help reduce prospect and customer frustration, it is a good practice to find a theme that loads quickly.

Support

Before choosing an e-commerce theme, it is a good idea to research the technical support that will be available in case you need it. Whether this support is available on YouTube, user forums, or the theme creator's website, it needs to be readily accessible and accurate.

Clean and Multipage Layout

When choosing a theme for e-commerce or other purposes, a good principle to follow is the K.I.S.S. Principle: Keep It Simple Silly. Visitors prefer a simple and clean layout that is easy to navigate and use. A clean and simple design also helps the theme and its pages load faster. It is important to remember that although a theme might be attractive, it serves no purpose if visitors cannot easily use and navigate it intuitively.

Theme Examples

Now that some of the things to look for when evaluating themes have been discussed, let's look at some examples.

8Store

8Store is a free WordPress-WooCommerce responsive theme that is suitable for business use (Figure 5-9).

Figure 5-9. *8Store free WordPress-WooCommerce theme*

Sold from Dessign.net

The Sold theme is another free WooCommerce responsive theme with a clean and minimal design (Figure 5-10).

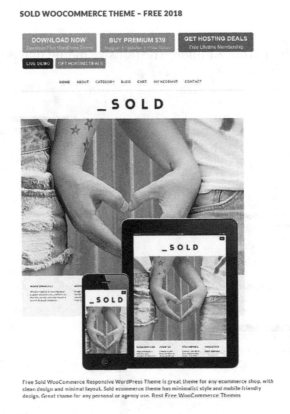

Figure 5-10. *Sold WooCommerce theme*

E-commerce Gem

The e-commerce Gem theme is available for download at `www.wordpress.org`
(Figure 5-11). According to Wordpress.org, it is a multipurpose theme that can be used
for all types of e-commerce websites and any store type. According to the Wordpress.org
website, the e-commerce Gem theme's features consist of "product search with category
select, multiple sections on the front page, full width easy to use slider, latest and
featured product carousel, call to actions, advertisement section, banners and more."[7]

---

[7]`https://wordpress.org/themes/ecommerce-gem/`

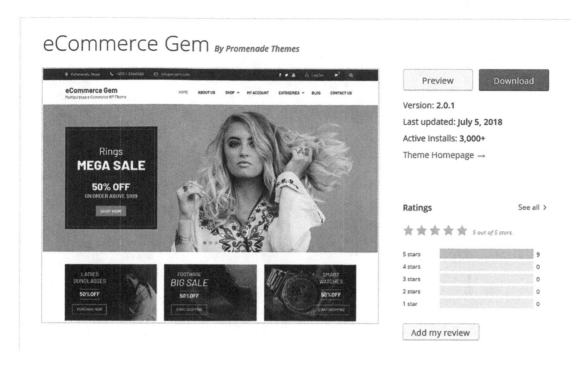

Figure 5-11. *E-commerce Gem theme*

Unlike brick and mortar stores, sales associates are not walking around to greet and assist customers who might need help. Although providing customer service via online chat might be available, it is still not the same as personal face-to-face attention.

Summary

Before launching any e-commerce store, it is imperative that the customer experience be carefully considered and planned. When it comes to an online store, the saying, "you never get a second chance to make a first impression" is true. With the advances in social media, a negative customer experience can spread over the Internet like a wildfire and impact whether future customers will visit the store. Choosing an e-commerce theme should not be taken lightly because it forms the basis for a successful or unsuccessful store and customer experience. It is always a good idea to think about what potential customers would like to see upon entering an online store and build from there.

CHAPTER 6

Creating Your Online Store

In Chapter 5, you learned about e-commerce themes, their benefits, and how they can help your business create an attractive online storefront. You also reviewed the features that you should consider before selecting a theme. Not all themes are created equal, and not all themes serve the same purpose. It is good practice to choose a theme from a category that closely matches your business's industry. Since we will be using WooCommerce to create your online store, we look at the Storefront theme, which is the default theme for WooCommerce and how it can help set up your online store and extend its features with its popular extensions.

Now it's time for the rubber to hit the road and begin creating your online store with WooCommerce. Most people are ready to dive right in and start adding products or services, but organization is key for long-term growth and success. Depending on the number of products your company plans to sell, it is always a good idea to start off by creating categories.

Product or Service Categories

Let's face it. Whether shopping in-store or online, many consumers do not want to aimlessly search for what they want or need. Why? They are inpatient and in a hurry. Upon arriving at a brick and mortar or online store, many already know what they need to purchase but just need to locate it and pay for it. If you picture yourself in your favorite brick and mortar store, what are some things that help you quickly locate the items that you need? A helpful and friendly sales associate? Familiarity with the store's layout? Stores such as Walmart or Target have good signage at the beginning of each aisle to help customers find or come close to finding what they need. In a 2014 article on managingissues.com, it addressed why women prefer shopping at Lowe's over

© Lisa Sims 2018
L. Sims, *Building Your Online Store With WordPress and WooCommerce*,
https://doi.org/10.1007/978-1-4842-3846-2_6

its competitor, Home Depot. The reasoning is simple: cleanliness and organization. According to the article, Home Depot stores can be described in the following way.

> The Home Depot is a bit messy. Tradesmen are walking about in work clothes and there are folk[sic] trucks in the isles filled with pallets that look like they can topple over onto a passerby at a moment's notice. The experience can be a tad intimidating for someone who is unfamiliar with such a masculine' environment.

> Lowes, on the other hand, is bright and shiny. Floors are freshly-waxed, a member of staff greets customers at the entrance and directs them to the products they are most interested in finding. It is a welcoming experience, one that many women may prefer when compared to THD.[1]

Besides selecting an attractive e-commerce theme, adding descriptive categories is another way to provide a welcoming customer experience. With WooCommerce installed, you can either run the Setup Wizard or Skip setup. For our purposes, we will walk through the Setup Wizard.

Setup Wizard

The WooCommerce Setup Wizard allows you to configure basic settings through a guided screen by a screen walk-through of five setup components:

- Page Setup
- Store location
- Shipping
- Payments
- Themes

This section can also be completed within the WordPress Dashboard. Let's look at these settings.

---

[1]http://www.management-issues.com/opinion/6965/how-appealing-to-women-has-helped-the-home-depot/

Page Setup

WooCommerce requires several essential pages:

- Shop – The shop page will display your products.

- Cart – The cart page will be where the customers go to view their cart and begin checkout.

- Checkout – The checkout page will be where the customers go to pay for their items.

- My account – Registered customers will be able to manage their account details and view past orders on this page.

Some of these pages might be duplicated if moving from another shopping cart, so it is a good idea to remove any previous shopping cart pages that might exist to avoid a potential conflict. For a first-time WooCommerce installation, these pages will not exist and will automatically be created. These pages can be managed from the admin dashboard on the pages screen.

Store Setup

The Store setup screen allows you to provide basic information about your store such as where your store is based along with whether physical, digital, or a combination of both will be sold (Figure 6-1). If unsure about what types of products will be sold and to save time in the future, it would probably be good to select the option for both physical and digital products. If you plan on selling products or services in person, don't forget to select the checkbox. If you would like to help improve WooCommerce, you can also select the checkbox to allow user tracking. You can always change this information in the WordPress Dashboard under WooCommerce ➤ Settings ➤ General Tab. Once everything is completed, click on the Let's Go button.

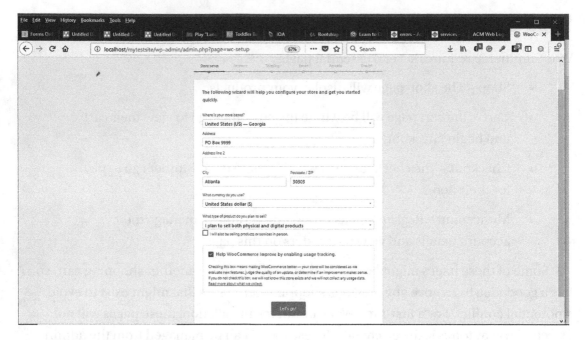

Figure 6-1. *Store setup in WooCommerce Setup Wizard*

Payment

The next step in the Setup Wizard is to setup your online store's payment options (Figure 6-2). WooCommerce allows Stripe, PayPal, and others that can be added later. WooCommerce also allows other payment options such as:

- Offline payments
- Check payments
- Bank transfer payment
- Cash on delivery

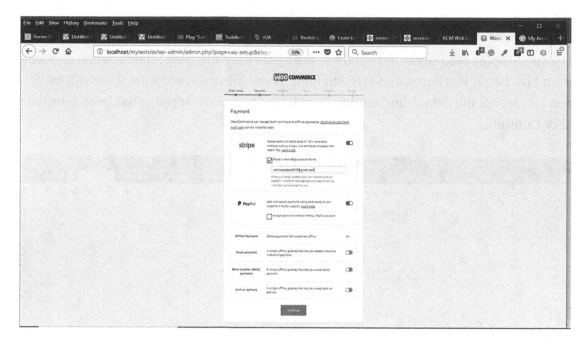

Figure 6-2. *Configuring payment options in WooCommerce*

In the WooCommerce Settings Checkout Tab, the various checkout methods are available to be configured. If you choose to use another payment gateway in addition to PayPal, you will need an SSL Certificate. What is an SSL Certificate? According to networksolutions.com, an SSL Certificate (Secure Sockets Layer), "also called a Digital Certificate, creates a secure link between a website and a visitor's browser. By ensuring that all data passed between the two remains private and secure, SSL encryption prevents hackers from stealing private information such as credit card numbers, names and addresses."[2] Online shoppers expect to see "https" in their address bar or a lock in the status bar indicating that their transaction will be secure. With so many data breaches occurring in the news, shoppers are concerned about the security of their financial information. SSL certificates are available for free (unless you prefer the green bar) from certificate authorities such as Let's Encrypt SSL or COMODO AutoSSL, which are equally recognized by Google, banks, and others. They can also be purchased from your web hosting provider or other providers such as namecheap.com, networksolutions.com, and others.

---

[2]http://www.networksolutions.com/education/what-is-an-ssl-certificate/

81

Shipping

On the shipping tab (Figure 6-3), you can configure your shipping rates. You can choose from Live Rates, Flat Rates, and Free Shipping. If you are unsure of what these will be, you can accept the default and modify them later. Once your shipping has been selected, click Continue.

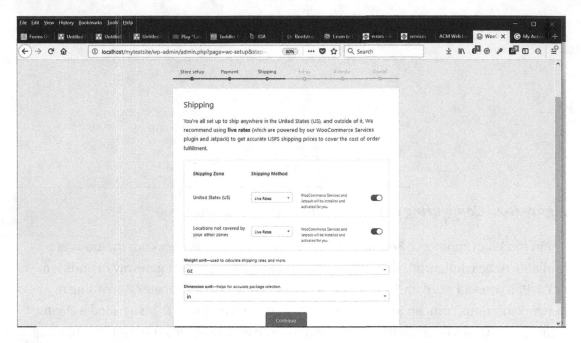

Figure 6-3. *Shipping tab of the WooCommerce Setup Wizard*

Recommended Extras

If you have installed the Storefront Theme as your default theme, it will be indicated here, and you can choose to install it (Figure 6-4). You can also choose the option for automating taxes so that you do not have to worry about it.

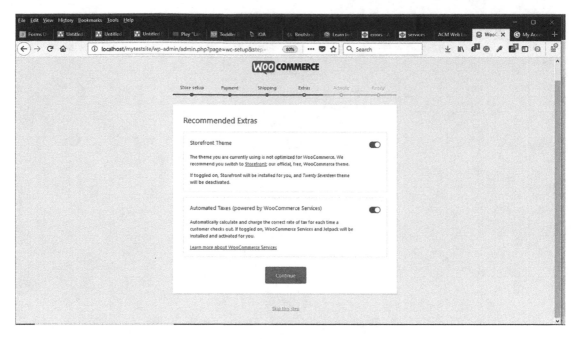

Figure 6-4. *Installing recommended extras in Setup Wizard*

Activate

On the Activate tab, you can choose to connect the JetPack plugin, which provides extra benefits to help with your online store (Figure 6-5). You can always skip this step and install it later. If you want to take advantage of automated tax calculations, live shipping rates, and product ratings, you will need to connect the JetPack. Once you have decided, click Continue.

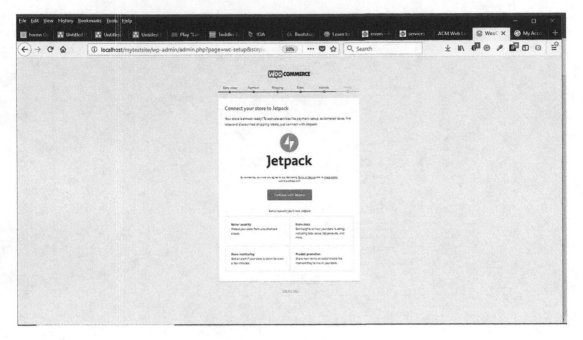

Figure 6-5. *Activate tab of Setup Wizard*

Ready

The Ready Tab allows you to sign up for WooCommerce email updates (Figure 6-6). You can also watch guided videos of WooCommerce and visit the WooCommerce website to find more information about getting started. The next step is to either create products or import products from an existing store via a CSV file. We will discuss how to import products from an existing CSV file later in the chapter. For now, click on the Create Products button to continue setting up your store.

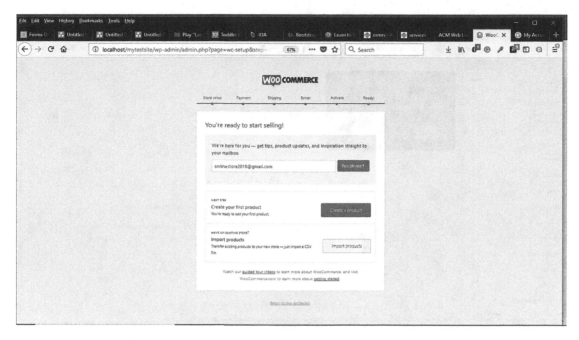

Figure 6-6. *Ready tab of the Setup Wizard*

After successfully completing the WooCommerce Setup Wizard, it is time to start creating your store.

Creating Your Store

In the WordPress Dashboard, WooCommerce presents an option to create a homepage based on the Storefront theme as well as add example products. Adding example products is a good way to learn tips and tricks for adding your products. These example products can always be deleted before your store launches. You can either leave the checkboxes selected and click the Let's Go button or begin adding products. Each method will be demonstrated. The Let's go option will be explored first.

After clicking the Let's Go button, you can begin customizing your store. The Customizer tool will walk you through each of the store options on the left (Figure 6-7). If you choose to skip the Customizer, you can always access it from the WordPress Dashboard by clicking WooCommerce ➤ Settings. As you can see (Figure 6-8), the Active theme is the Storefront Theme. To change to another installed theme or choose from one of the WordPress themes, click the Change button.

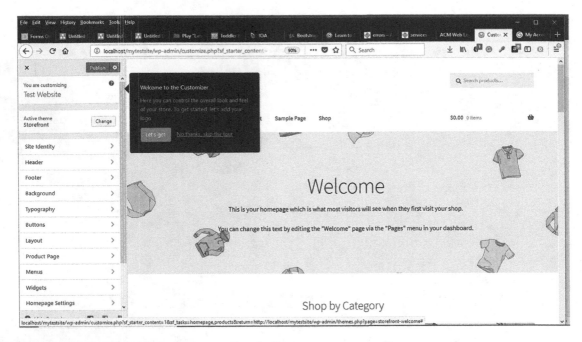

Figure 6-7. *The Customizer tool to help set up your online store*

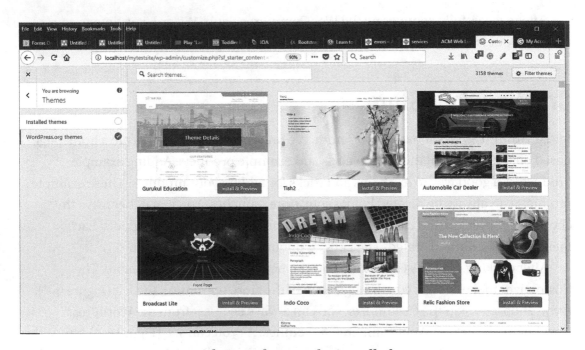

Figure 6-8. *The WordPress themes that can be installed*

Site Identity

Establishing your store's identity or brand is a crucial first step when creating your online store (Figure 6-9). When potential customers visit your store for the first time, you want them to immediately know who you are and begin to recognize your logo. If you don't have a logo, you can use free tools such as Canva.com or the free open source graphics program, GIMP, to create a logo. You can also hire a freelancer on Fiverr.com to create a logo starting at $5. WordPress recommends logo dimensions of 470 by 110 pixels. For the Site Title, use the name of your store. To give visitors a good idea of what your store is about, it is a good idea to provide a short descriptive tagline that will appear underneath the Site Title. It is also a good idea to provide a site icon for your store to help reinforce your store's identity and brand.

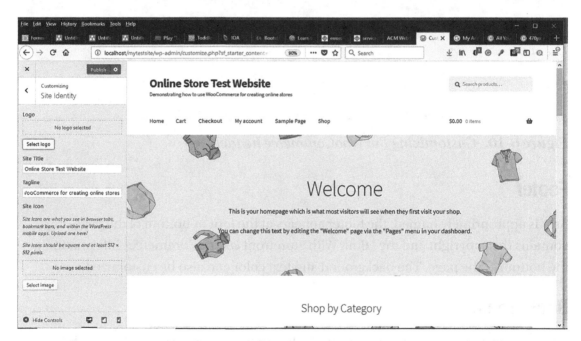

Figure 6-9. *Configuring the Site Identity information for an online store*

Header

The header background image can also help to reinforce your brand to visitors and create a good first impression. The Storefront theme recommends a background image size of 1950 by 500 pixels (Figure 6-10). Once the header image is uploaded, you can either crop it or not. If you choose not to use a header image, you can choose a header background color instead along with changing the text and link color. You want to make sure that your color selections are pleasing to the eye and complement each other nicely.

Figure 6-10. *Customizing the WooCommerce header*

Footer

As it is appropriately named, the footer appears at the foot or bottom of the page. It contains the copyright and the "Built With Storefront & WooCommerce" information at the bottom of the page. The background and text color can also be customized.

Background

Like with the header image, you can also include a background image along with the background color. Pay careful attention to your color selections so that they don't distract from your products and the brand of your store.

Typography, Buttons

In these sections, the only attribute that can be customized is their colors.

Layout

Within this section, you can select from one of the two available general layouts: right and left (Figure 6-11).

Figure 6-11. *Selecting the general layout of your store*

Product Page

On the Product Page, the Sticky-Add-To-Cart and Product Pagination options are selected by default (Figure 6-12). According to the WooCommerce website, a Sticky Add-To-Cart display a small content bar at the top of the browser window that includes relevant product information and an add-to-cart button. It slides into view once the standard add-to-cart button has scrolled out of view. Potential customers and customers need to be able to always add items to their cart.

Product pagination allows for previous and next buttons to be displayed when there are many products available instead of having visitors continuously scrolling. It is a good practice to keep these selected. If you feel that you will not need them, you can always deselect them later.

For downloadable products, additional settings can be configured from the WooCommerce Settings page by selecting Products ➤ Downloadable Products (Figure 6-13).

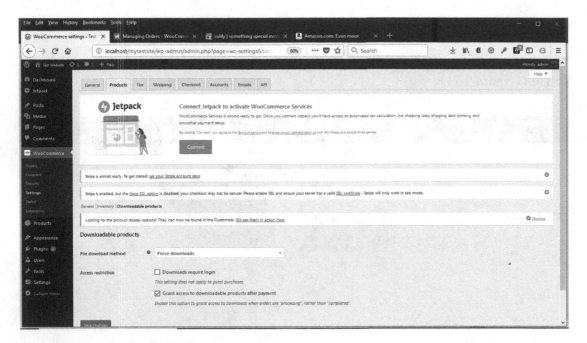

Figure 6-12. *Settings for downloadable products in WooCommerce Setting Page*

Figure 6-13. *Product Page in WooCommerce*

Menus

Menus are a great way to allow visitors to navigate your store. Since most visitors are already familiar with using menus to navigate online stores, they will not have much of a learning curve. To create a new menu, click on the create menu button (Figure 6-14).

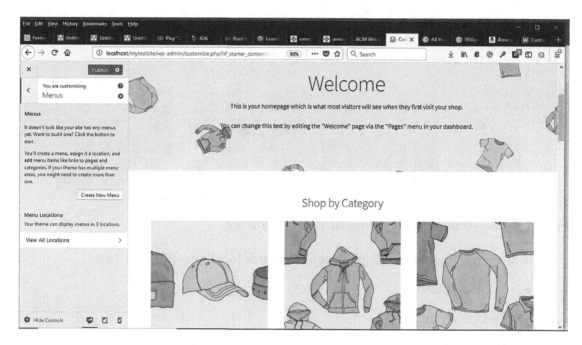

***Figure 6-14.** Menu option within WooCommerce*

When creating menus, it is a good practice to give them descriptive names so that visitors can easily navigate them, and the manager of the store can easily modify them (Figure 6-15). Menu locations can also be specified.

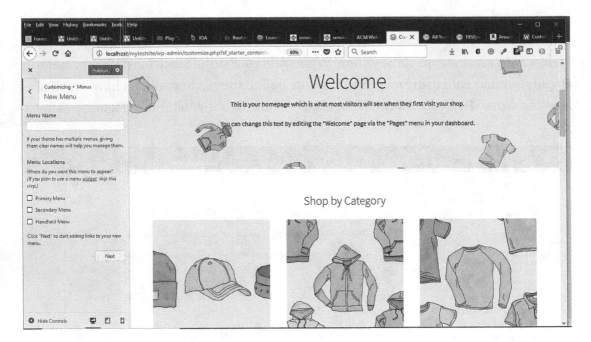

Figure 6-15. *New menu location in WooCommerce*

The Storefront theme can display menus in three locations (Figure 6-16):

- Primary menu

- Secondary menu

- Handheld menu

Figure 6-16. *Menu View All Locations in WooCommerce*

Widgets

As previously discussed in Chapter 3, widgets easily add functionality to an online store without requiring any coding knowledge. Certain widgets can be installed in the header and footer sections (Figure 6-17). Some of these widgets will be explored later in the chapter. There are four locations on the footer along with the one below the header and on the sidebar where widgets can be installed. What types of widgets can be installed? According to the WooCommerce website, these are the default widgets that can be installed:

- Active Product Filters – Display a list of active filters.

- Filter Products by Attribute – Display a list of attributes to filter products in your store.

- Filter Products by Price – Display a slider to filter products in your store by price.

- Filter Products by Rating – Display a list of star ratings to filter products in your store.

- Product Categories – A list or drop-down of product categories.

- Products – A list of your store's products.

- Products by Rating – A list of your store's top-rated products.

- Product Search – A search form for your store.

- Product Tag Cloud – A cloud of your most used product tags.

- Recent Product Reviews – Display a list of recent reviews from your store.

- Recent Viewed Products – Display a list of a customer's recently viewed products.

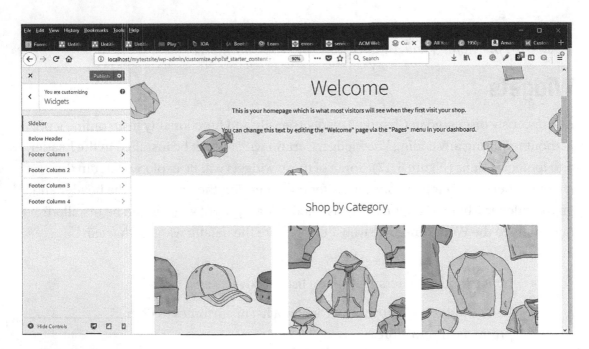

Figure 6-17. *Adding widgets in WooCommerce*

Homepage Settings

First impressions are lasting impressions. Sometimes, you do not get a second chance to make a good first impression. Determining what visitors see upon arriving at your online store's homepage is vital. It can result in increased click-throughs of your store or an increased abandoned rate from visitors leaving the store. The homepage can be configured to display a static page or your recent blog posts (Figure 6-18).

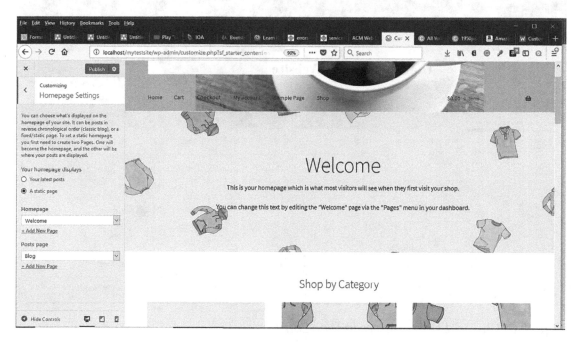

Figure 6-18. *Homepage settings in the WooCommerce Customizer*

Store Notice

WooCommerce makes it easy to manage your online store. You can enable a custom store notice message to be displayed to visitors by selecting a checkbox (Figure 6-19). Examples of information that could be displayed include downtime for support, addition of new products, and more.

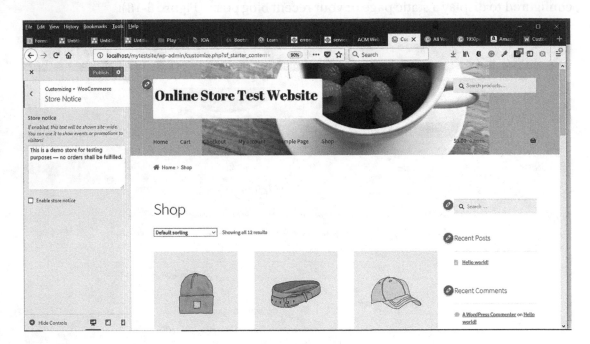

Figure 6-19. *Add store notices in WooCommerce*

Product Catalog

The product catalog section gives you complete control over how your online store will look (Figure 6-20). You can customize the shop page and category display, default product sorting, products per row, and row per page.

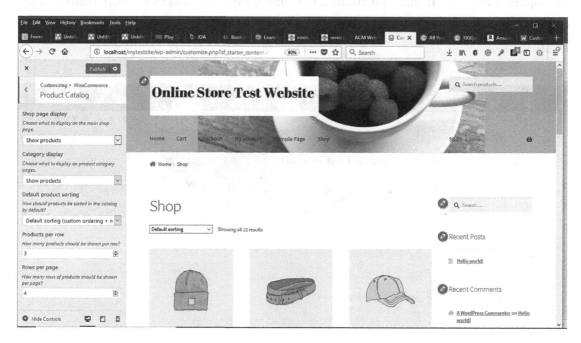

Figure 6-20. *Product catalog in WooCommerce*

WooCommerce

Product images allow potential customers to see your products or services and make decisions as to whether they want to learn more. Thumbnails are smaller images of your products or services displayed to users before they click on the product or service to see the bigger image and more information. Within the Product Images section, thumbnail cropping options can be selected to determine how thumbnail images will be cropped (Figure 6-21).

Figure 6-21. *Thumbnail cropping options in the Product Images*

Additional CSS

If you have your own cascading style sheet (CSS) that you would like to use, WooCommerce allows you to add it in the Additional CSS section (Figure 6-22). You can also learn more about CSS.

Figure 6-22. *Additional CSS in WooCommerce*

More

WooCommerce makes it easy to learn more about available Storefront extensions to enhance your online store (Figure 6-23). Within the WordPress Dashboard, visit the Storefront page for more information.

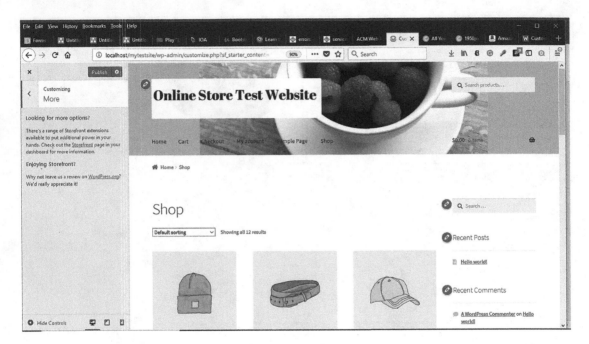

Figure 6-23. *More Options in the Customizer*

WooCommerce Settings

Now that we've gone through the Customizer, let's look at the WooCommerce Settings page where you will spend most of your time configuring your store.

General Tab

If you used the initial WooCommerce Setup Wizard, you completed this step in the Store Setup tab. If you skipped the Setup Wizard or need to change any information, you can do so on the General Tab (Figure 6-24). The General Tab contains store-specific information such as the address, selling and shipping locations, and tax and currency information.

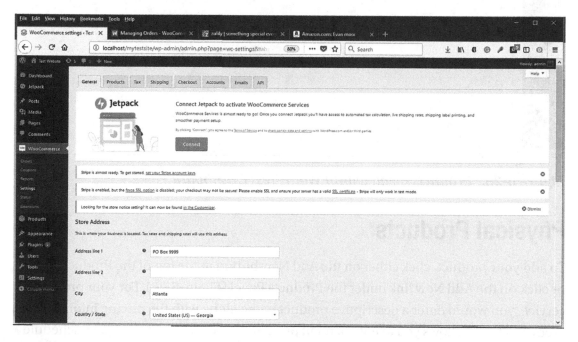

Figure 6-24. *General tab in WooCommerce Settings*

Products

The Products menu (Figure 6-25) within the WordPress Dashboard is where products are added or modified.

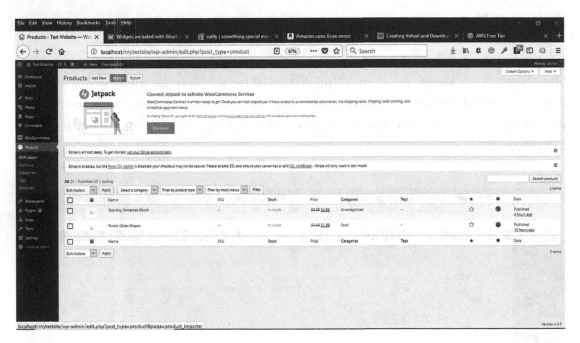

Figure 6-25. *Products menu within WordPress Dashboard*

Physical Products

To add your product, click either on the Add New button at the top of the Products Page or click on the Add New link under the Products Panel (Figure 6-26). For your product or service, you would enter a descriptive product name along with the pricing information. WooCommerce allows you to enter a retail price and a sale price. You can also schedule the sale price duration. Once your product is created, you can either add it to an existing category or create a new one. If you decide to create a new category, you can add it to an existing Parent category such as adding socks to a shoes parent category. You can also add a product image as well as product tags. It is a good practice to provide descriptive tags for your products to help people locate your products. Likewise, it is also good to include descriptive keywords when you are naming your images. Providing good quality images can also help potential customers make informed decisions as to whether to purchase your products. Make sure that you use a good high-quality resolution camera along with good lighting when taking product pictures or hire a good photographer.

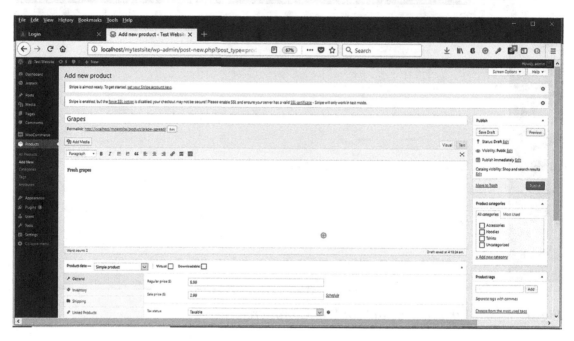

Figure 6-26. *Add New Product Page*

Virtual Products

Virtual products are products that are downloaded rather than shipped. They are intangible. Virtual products consist of e-books, PDF documents, music, services, and more. When adding these products on the Add New Product page (Figure 6-27), clicking the virtual checkbox indicates that they are virtual products and no shipping is involved. When the virtual checkbox is selected, the shipping option is not available.

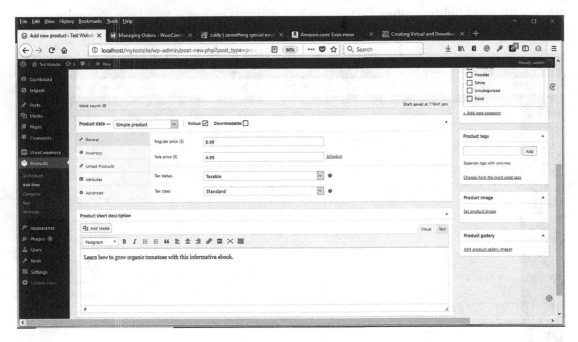

Figure 6-27. *Virtual products in WooCommerce*

Downloadable Products

Downloadable products are a form of virtual products that have a file available for download after a completed purchase. These products would include e-books, music, PDF documents, and more. The shipping option is still not available. The downloadable and virtual checkboxes must be clicked to display the other downloadable information that needs to be completed such as downloadable files, download limit, and the download expiration (Figure 6-28). It is a good practice to give your downloadable products descriptive names so that customers have an idea of what they are downloading. Likewise, consider using a cloud-based storage such as Amazon's S3 for storing your files. Depending on the number of downloadable files you have, you could qualify for an Amazon S3 free-tier account (expires 12 months after sign-up), which includes 5GB of storage, 20,000 Get Requests, and 2,000 Put Requests. For more information, visit `https://aws.amazon.com`.

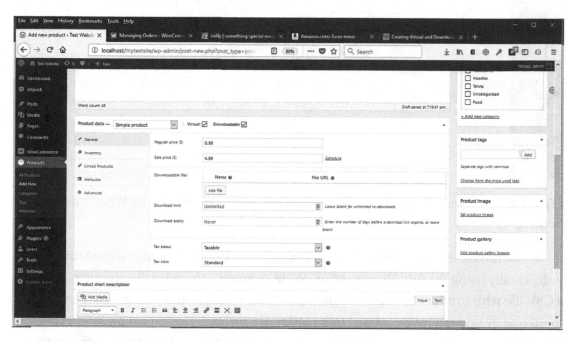

Figure 6-28. *Downloadable product page in WooComerce*

Once your downloadable products have been added, you can specify their download method and set their access restrictions on the downloadable products area of the Products Tab in WooCommerce Settings (Figure 6-29).

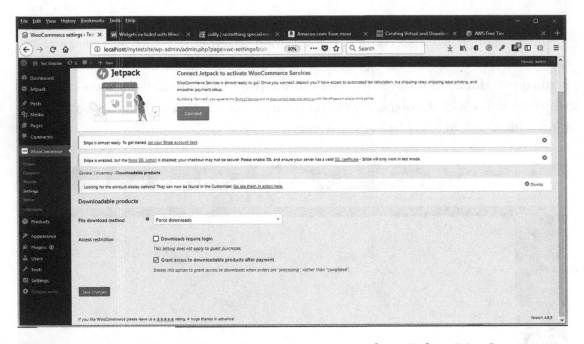

Figure 6-29. *Downloadable products section on Products Tab in WooCommerce Settings*

If you have a large inventory of products, it can be time consuming to add them individually using the Add New function. WooCommerce provides the ability to import a CSV file with product information into your store, which is much faster than entering them one by one. There is a wizard that guides you through the import process. A sample CSV file format for products is available on the WooCommerce documentation website.

Inventory

WooCommerce makes it easy to manage your store's inventory. The last thing you want is to have a customer ready to buy products, but they are out of stock. Clicking on the inventory link will allow you to add a product SKU, manage stock, set stock status, or indicate whether a product can be sold individually. Indicating that you want to manage stock will make stock quantity and allow backorder options available. If you are unclear of what an option means, you can click on the question mark beside the option. More advanced inventory settings can be configured in the WooCommerce Settings (Figure 6-30).

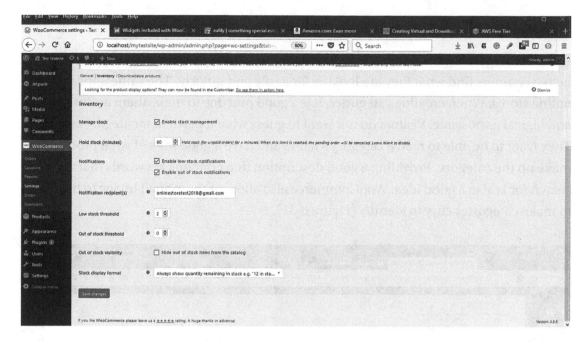

Figure 6-30. *Inventory settings in WooCommerce Settings section*

Shipping

As you are adding your products, you can also configure shipping information. In this section, you would enter your products' weights and dimensions. Once you connect to JetPack, you can take advantage of the live rate settings. In development mode, this information is not available.

Linked Products

By choosing the linked products option, you can either upsell or cross-sell your products.

Categories

Product categories are similar to the aisle signage in grocery stores or retail stores. They help customers find what they are looking for easily and quickly. The same applies to online stores. When creating categories, it is a good practice to make them as descriptive and logical as possible. Visitors do not want to guess what a particular category contains. They want to be able to read a category's name and have a good idea of what products make up the category. Providing a good description that contains keywords that visitors search for is also a good idea. WooCommerce also allows a thumbnail image to be added to make categories easy to identify (Figure 6-31).

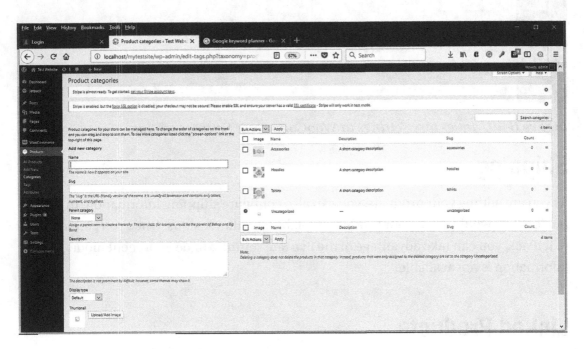

Figure 6-31. *Product categories for WooCommerce*

Product Tags

When creating your products, product tags are extremely important. Product tags allow you to create user-friendly URLs that can contain keywords about your products (Figure 6-32). This helps your products to be discovered in various search engines such as Google or Bing. Most people will find your store via search engines, so why not add descriptive keyword tags to your products? Not sure what keywords or phrases people are using to search for your products? Google Keyword Planner is an excellent free resource that will help you find the search terms that people are using.

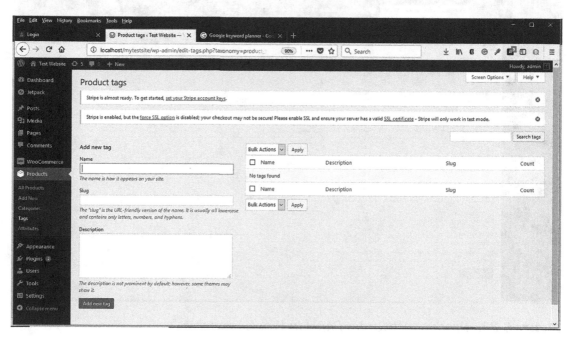

Figure 6-32.   *Product Tags Panel in WooCommerce*

Attributes

Depending on the type of products, additional information might be needed to help customers complete their selections (Figure 6-33). For example, when purchasing clothing such as shirts or pants, customers must be able to select the color and size. WooCommerce's attributes panel is where this information would be specified. You can also set the default sorting order for these attributes, which is helpful for items such as sizes and colors.

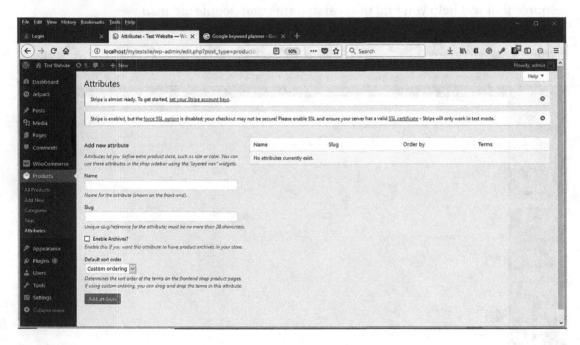

Figure 6-33. *Product Attributes Panel in WooCommerce*

Orders

To view orders that you receive, Select WooCoomerce ➤ Orders (Figure 6-34). All orders will appear within the area with the shopping cart. Since no orders have been placed, this page initially appears empty. WooCommerce offers more information on orders by clicking on the Learn more about orders button. We will discuss order management in Chapters 9 and 10.

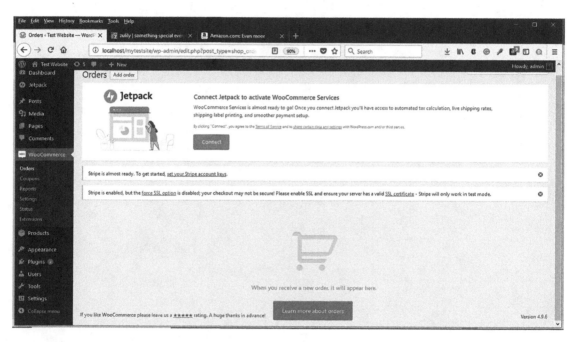

Figure 6-34. *Orders page of WooCommerce*

Summary

Setting up an online store with WooCommerce is not as daunting of a task as some might think. With its various Setup Wizards and Customizer Wizard serving as guides along the way, an online store can be set up quickly. By planning what products will be sold as well as their categories, visitors can experience a good first shopping experience that can turn them into repeat customers. In the next chapter, we'll explore securing your online store.

CHAPTER 7

Securing Your Online Store

In the previous chapter, The WooCommerce Setup Wizard was illustrated along with how to configure its settings within the WordPress Dashboard according to a store's specifications. It also explored how to add products and services to a WooCommerce store as well as assign them to the appropriate categories along with other inventory management settings. Throughout the chapter, many e-commerce best practices were discussed to help give visitors and customers a pleasant and memorable shopping experience.

Once products and services and other information have been added to an online store, many store owners are ready to launch. However, before launching it to the world, there are certain precautions that must be done to make sure it is secure. Security must be a top priority.

With all the data breaches occurring in the news with brick and mortar and click and mortar stores as well as online stores lately, consumers are apprehensive whenever shopping in-store or online with their credit or debit cards. It is the uncertainty of not knowing what will happen to their personal and financial information once their transactions are completed. Not only does this affect consumers, but it also affects store owners because they are also consumers and experience similar concerns and feelings.

Consumers want to feel assured that a business has implemented the necessary security measures to protect and secure their personal and financial information from hackers and are constantly reviewing and updating them. Although some store owners might think that a security breach could not happen to their store, it could not be further from the truth. No one or any business is exempt. As the adage says, "Hope for the best but prepare for the worst." Murphy's Law states it this way: Whatever can go wrong, will go wrong. This chapter will present some best practices for not only securing an online store and reducing chances of a lawsuit but also securing customers' information.

© Lisa Sims 2018
L. Sims, *Building Your Online Store With WordPress and WooCommerce*,
https://doi.org/10.1007/978-1-4842-3846-2_7

Security Strategies

Security strategies are crucial for an online store's success. Many of these strategies should be considered early in the planning phase so that they can be properly planned and implemented. During the busyness of setting up an online store, it can be easy for certain security strategies to be overlooked. By having these security strategies readily available, online store owners can be more proactive rather than reactive when a security breach occurs.

SSL Certificates

When shopping online, consumers feel that they can trust a company if they see any of these items on their website:

- Lock icon to the left of URL name

- "https" in browser address bar instead of "http"

- Certificating Authority Trust seal

- Green address bar (for an EV SSL Certificate)

These items represent that a website has an SSL Certificate or digital certificate. Certain browsers such as Google Chrome will display all websites as unsecure when an SSL certificate is not used.[1] What is a Secure Socket Layer (SSL)? According to Verisign,[2] one of the leaders in domain names and Internet Security, describes SSL as follows:

> . . . a global standard security technology that enables encrypted communication between a web browser and a web server. It is utilized by millions[1] of online businesses and individuals to decrease the risk of sensitive information (e.g., credit card numbers, usernames, passwords, emails, etc.) from being stolen or tampered with by hackers and identity thieves. In essence, SSL allows for a private "conversation" just between the two intended parties.

---

[1]https://searchengineland.com/effective-july-2018-googles-chrome-browser-will-mark-non-https-sites-as-not-secure-291623

[2]https://www.verisign.com/en_US/website-presence/website-optimization/ssl-certificates/index.xhtml

Most people think that SSL is only used to secure online financial information, but it is also used to secure any confidential or sensitive information such as:

- Medical records

- Logins and passwords

- Legal documents and contracts

- Proprietary information

- Personal data

- Client lists

Typically, SSL certificates are issued by Certificate Authorities (CAs) who accept applications but can also be purchased from domain registrars and web hosting providers. Not all SSL Certificates are the same and depend on the number of domains or subdomains a company wants to secure. SSL consists of two components: SSL type and validation. Although there are many SSL types, Verisign describes the top three as:

- **Single** – secures one fully qualified domain name or subdomain name.

- **Wildcard** – secures one domain name and an unlimited number of its subdomains.

- **Multi-domain** – secures multiple domain names.

Verisign also describes the level of validation as the following:

- **Domain Validation** – This level is the least expensive and covers basic encryption and verification of the ownership of the domain name registration. This type of certificate usually takes a few minutes to several hours to receive.

- **Organization Validation** – In addition to basic encryption and verification of ownership of the domain name registration, certain details of the owner (e.g., name and address) are authenticated. This type of certificate usually takes a few hours to several days to receive.

- **Extended Validation (EV)** – This provides the highest degree of
  security because of the thorough examination that is conducted
  before this certificate is issued (and as strictly specified in guidelines
  set by the SSL certification industry's governing consortium). In
  addition to ownership of the domain name registration and entity
  authentication, the legal, physical, and operational existence of the
  entity is verified. This type of certificate usually takes a few days to
  several weeks to receive.

Most small businesses will utilize a single SSL type along with domain validation,
but it depends on the business's needs. On the Checkout Tab in WooCommerce, there
is an option to select whether to force secure checkout (Figure 7-1). WooCommerce
recommends running an entire website/store with https and not just the checkout page.
Once force secure checkout is selected, another option becomes available to force HTTP
when the visitor leaves checkout. To enter an SSL Certificate or sign up for a free one,
click on an SSL Certificate is required hyperlink (Figure 7-2).

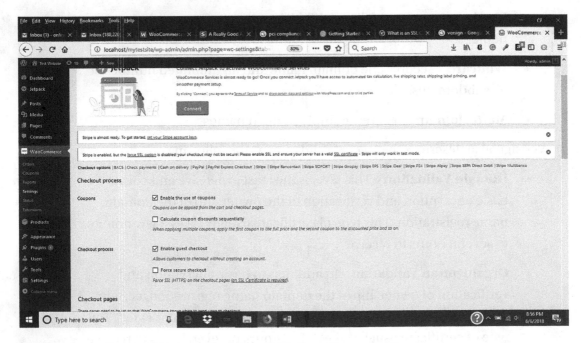

Figure 7-1. *Forcing SSL and adding SSL Certificate in WooCommerce*

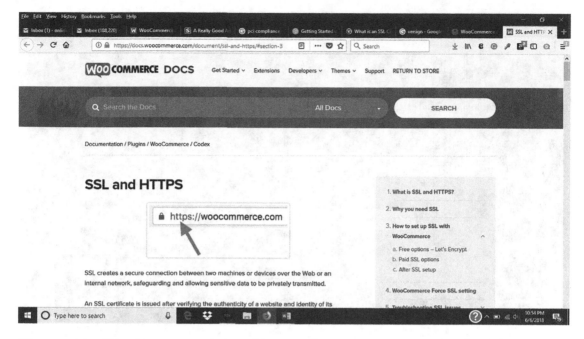

Figure 7-2. *WooCommerce instructions on how to set up a free and paid SSL and HTTPS*

Free SSL Certificates can be obtained from Let's Encrypt (`https://letsencrypt.org/`). "Let's Encrypt" is a certificate authority (CA) that issues SSL certificates. WooCommerce hosting partners such as Bluehost, Pressable, and SiteGround provide free SSL certificates for WordPress users to install with a few clicks. These certificates are domain based. If using other web hosting, it is a good idea to ask whether they offer free SSL certificates.

To manually install an SSL certificate on a web server, follow these steps:

1. Purchase a domain name from a registrar. Remember that the Let's Encrypt free SSL certificates are domain based.

2. Purchase web hosting from a web hosting provider.

3. Go to `www.ZeroSSL.com` (Figure 7-3).

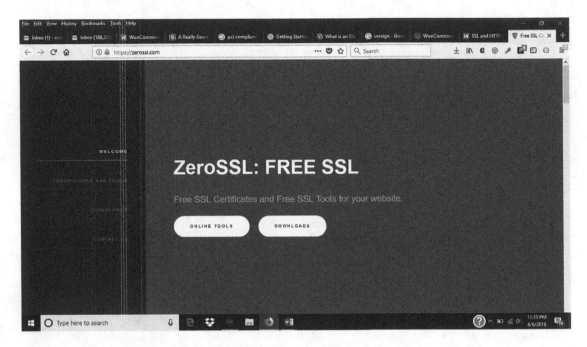

Figure 7-3. *Signing up for a free SSL at ZeroSSL*

    4.   Click on Certificates and Tools and click Start (Figure 7-4).

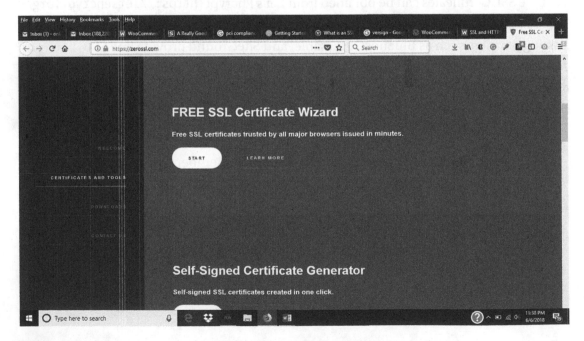

Figure 7-4. *Starting the process for Free SSL Certificate*

5.   Enter the domain name of your website and accept the **Terms
     of Service** (TOS), then select **Next** (Figure 7-5). This generates a
     Certificate Signing Request (CSR). If presented with "Include
     www-prefixed version too?," select Yes.

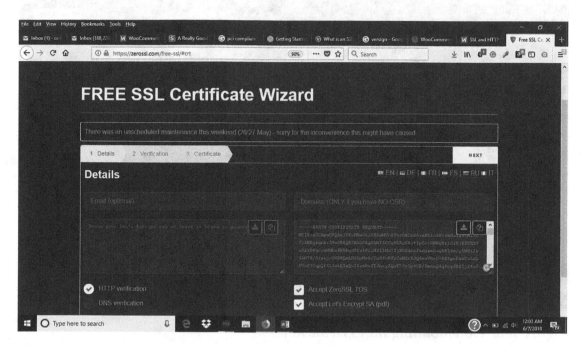

Figure 7-5. *Detail information for Free SSL Certificate Wizard*

6.   Download or copy the CSR.

7.   Select **Next** to generate your **RSA Private Key**.

8. Download your RSA Private Key. Make sure that you download
    both the CSR and the RSA Private Keys before closing the window.
    Otherwise, the process would have to be restarted (Figure 7-6).

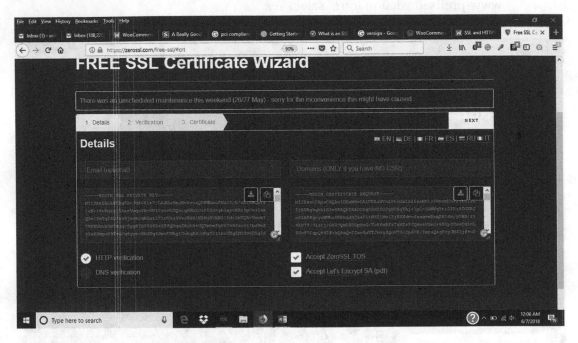

Figure 7-6. *Downloading RSA Private Key*

9. Contact the web hosting company for further instructions for
    uploading the generated free SSL.

After generating the CSR and RSA keys to install SSL, WordPress and WooCommerce
will need to be updated with the new URL in Settings (Figure 7-7).

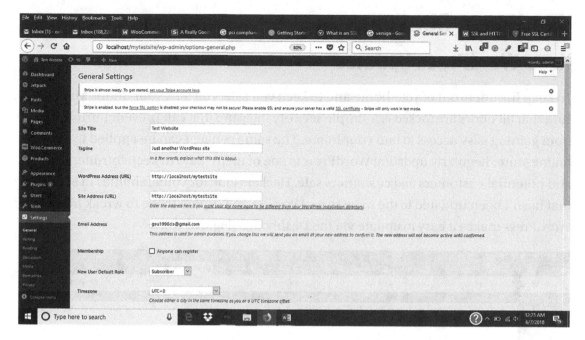

Figure 7-7. *Updating WordPress Address and Site Address after successful SSL installation*

PCI Compliance

Regardless of the payment processors selected, make sure that they are PCI compliant. What is PCI Compliance? The PCI Compliance Guide website states: "The Payment Card Industry Data Security Standard (PCI DSS) is a set of security standards designed to ensure that ALL companies that accept, process, store or transmit credit card information maintain a secure environment."[3] These standards apply to any business that accepts credit cards to help improve security while providing safety to consumers. A listing of PCI-compliant providers can be found on the PCI Compliance website (www.pcisecuritystandards.org).

---

[3]https://www.pcicomplianceguide.org/faq/#1

WordPress Strategies

Keep WordPress Updated

To keep intruders out of your home and to keep you safe, you lock your doors. Making sure that all doors are locked is a simple security measure that can prevent intruders from gaining easy access to into your home. The same concept can be applied to an online store. Regularly updating WordPress is one of many ways to keep intruders out and potential customers and customers safe. Hackers look for vulnerabilities in software that hasn't been updated to the most recent version and exploit those to wreak havoc. WordPress makes it easy to update via the Dashboard (Figure 7-8).

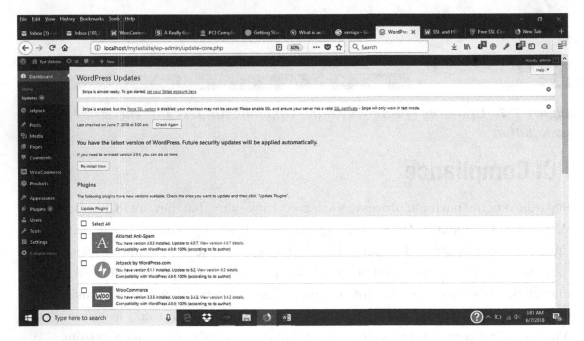

Figure 7-8. *Keeping WordPress updated via the WordPress dashboard*

Use Strong Passwords

A weak password is like leaving a key in a lock. They allow easy entry to a website when they shouldn't. It is good practice to use a strong password to help secure WordPress and WooCommerce. Passwords should be 8–14 characters long and consist of upper and lowercase letters, numbers, and special characters. It is also a good practice to not choose a password that is based on something personal or common knowledge that can be easily guessed.

Choose Reputable Web Hosts

For some, choosing a web host can be a daunting task because there are so many things to consider for a website's needs. When choosing a web host, it is a good practice to choose a reputable host who has been in business for a while and has good reviews. Getting referrals from others can help select a good web host. Besides referrals, what else can be done to find web hosts? On the WordPress and WooCommerce websites, they provide listings of reputable web hosts who support WordPress and WooCommerce.

Keep WordPress Plugins Updated

The same way that it is good to keep WordPress updated, it is also a good idea to keep WordPress and WooCommerce plugins updated. Plugins that have not been updated to newer versions can allow hackers to exploit vulnerabilities with the plugin that the newer version addresses. Newer versions of plugins can be released that add additional features and security. Plugins that are no longer used should be deleted to eliminate potential security breach opportunities.

JetPack Protect

JetPack Protect provides many features that can help secure websites and online stores. For security, it can help protect against unwanted brute force attacks, malware scanning, and spam filtering. It can also back up a website or online store in real time and alert owners via email and push notifications about downtime.

Change the Default "Admin" Username

When WordPress is initially installed, it creates an admin username. Hackers look for this username to try to obtain unauthorized access to conduct brute force attacks to a website. Store owners can either re-create another user account with a different username and delete the existing one or use a plugin such as Username Changer to change the admin username. Another option is to update the username in the MySQL database using myPHPadmin.

Change WordPress Database Prefix

By default, WordPress tables names are prefixed with wp_ in the underlying MySQL database. Hackers can use this to their advantage to guess a store's tables names. It is recommended that these table names be changed. Some web host such as Bluehost will take care of this during the WordPress installation. However, changing the table names could leave a store nonoperational until it is resolved, so it is best to back up your WordPress database with the BackupBuddy plugin or a similar one.

In the website root directory, locate the wp-config.php file and change the $table_ prefix to something that contains either numbers, letters, or underscores:

```
$table_prefix = 'wp_aug1234';
```

Next, open the database using phpMyAdmin to change the table names to the prefix used in the wp-config.php file. This is located within a web host's cPanel (Figure 7-9).

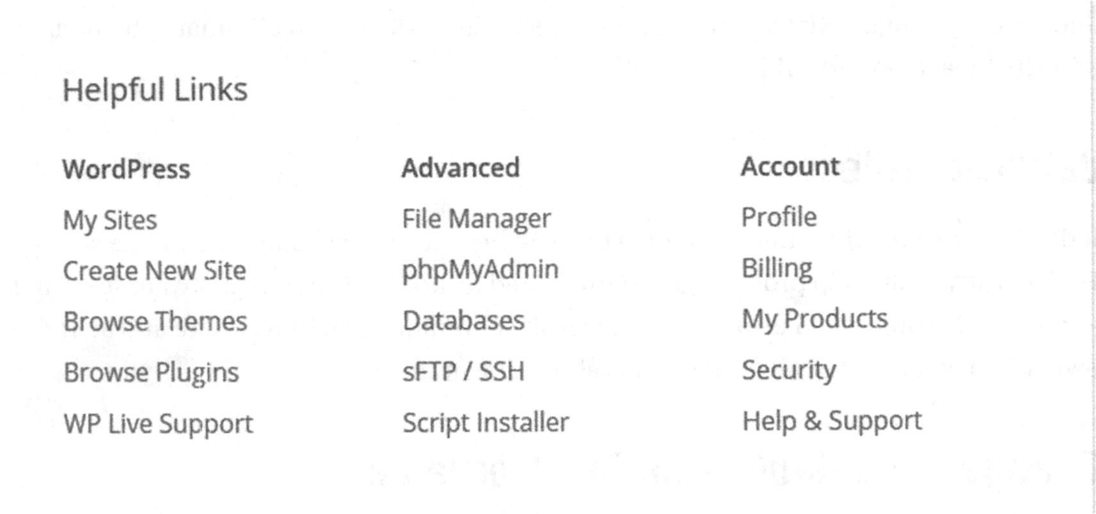

Helpful Links

WordPress	Advanced	Account
My Sites	File Manager	Profile
Create New Site	phpMyAdmin	Billing
Browse Themes	Databases	My Products
Browse Plugins	sFTP / SSH	Security
WP Live Support	Script Installer	Help & Support

Figure 7-9. *Accessing the phpMyAdmin through the cPanel*

There are 12 database tables that will need to be changed (Figure 7-10).

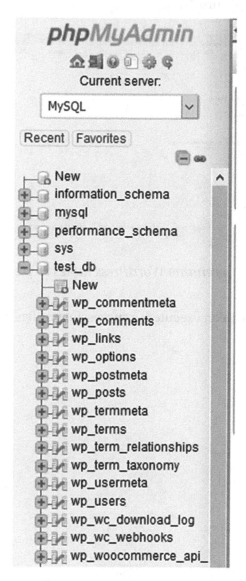

Figure 7-10. *WordPress tables in phpMyAdmin*

Instead of changing these 12 table names manually, an SQL script can be used to change them at one time (Figure 7-11).

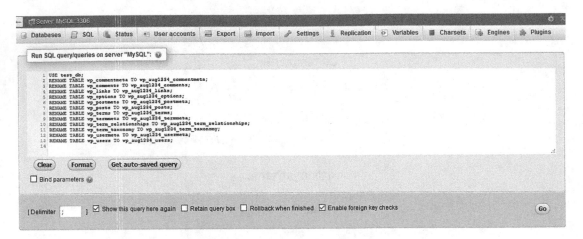

Figure 7-11. *SQL script to rename WordPress tables in phpMyAdmin*

Once the queries have been executed, a successful notification will be displayed (Figure 7-12).

MySQL returned an empty result set (i.e. zero rows). (Query took 0.0011 seconds.)

test_db

[Edit inline] [Edit] [Create PHP code]

MySQL returned an empty result set (i.e. zero rows). (Query took 0.0338 seconds.)

AME TABLE wp_commentmeta TO wp_aug1234_commentmeta

[Edit inline] [Edit] [Create PHP code]

MySQL returned an empty result set (i.e. zero rows). (Query took 0.0389 seconds.)

AME TABLE wp_comments TO wp_aug1234_comments

[Edit inline] [Edit] [Create PHP code]

MySQL returned an empty result set (i.e. zero rows). (Query took 0.0122 seconds.)

AME TABLE wp_links TO wp_aug1234_links

[Edit inline] [Edit] [Create PHP code]

MySQL returned an empty result set (i.e. zero rows). (Query took 0.0114 seconds.)

AME TABLE wp_options TO wp_aug1234_options

[Edit inline] [Edit] [Create PHP code]

MySQL returned an empty result set (i.e. zero rows). (Query took 0.0112 seconds.)

AME TABLE wp_postmeta TO wp_aug1234_postmeta

[Edit inline] [Edit] [Create PHP code]

MySQL returned an empty result set (i.e. zero rows). (Query took 0.0117 seconds.)

AME TABLE wp_posts TO wp_aug1234_posts

[Edit inline] [Edit] [Create PHP code]

MySQL returned an empty result set (i.e. zero rows). (Query took 0.0778 seconds.)

AME TABLE wp_terms TO wp_aug1234_terms

MySQL returned an empty result set (i.e. zero rows). (Query took 0.0778 seconds.)

AME TABLE wp_terms TO wp_aug1234_terms

[Edit inline] [Edit] [Create PHP code]

MySQL returned an empty result set (i.e. zero rows). (Query took 0.0116 seconds.)

AME TABLE wp_termmeta TO wp_aug1234_termmeta

[Edit inline] [Edit] [Create PHP code]

MySQL returned an empty result set (i.e. zero rows). (Query took 0.0116 seconds.)

AME TABLE wp_term_relationships TO wp_aug1234_term_relationships

[Edit inline] [Edit] [Create PHP code]

MySQL returned an empty result set (i.e. zero rows). (Query took 0.0123 seconds.)

AME TABLE wp_term_taxonomy TO wp_aug1234_term_taxonomy

[Edit inline] [Edit] [Create PHP code]

MySQL returned an empty result set (i.e. zero rows). (Query took 0.0251 seconds.)

AME TABLE wp_usermeta TO wp_aug1234_usermeta

[Edit inline] [Edit] [Create PHP code]

MySQL returned an empty result set (i.e. zero rows). (Query took 0.0115 seconds.)

AME TABLE wp_users TO wp_aug1234_users

[Edit inline] [Edit] [Create PHP code]

Figure 7-12. *MySQL notification of query results*

By changing the default WordPress prefix for tables, hackers will have to work a little harder to bring down the website.

Firewalls, Antivirus, and Antispam

What is a firewall? According to Cisco, a firewall is "is a network security device that monitors incoming and outgoing network traffic and decides whether to allow or block specific traffic based on a defined set of security rules."[4] It can be hardware, software, or both. Typically, a firewall serves a first line of defense against intruders.

Firewalls

WordPress provides many different firewall options to help protect a website. One of those options is the Wordfence plugin. Available in both free and premium versions, the Wordfence Premium plugin is a web application firewall that reduces the chances of being hacked. In addition to being a firewall, it acts as a malware scanner, live website traffic monitor (premium), country and IP blocker (premium), and uses other features to give website owners peace of mind that their website is being protected.

A web application firewall helps prevent and block malicious attacks to websites before they happen. A recommended free WAF plugin for WordPress is Sucuri Security. Once installed and activated, a firewall API key will be needed to configure and protect a website (Figure 7-13). Although the Sucuri Security plugin is free, the firewall is available for basic, professional, and business use for a fee.

---

[4] https://www.cisco.com/c/en/us/products/security/firewalls/what-is-a-firewall.html

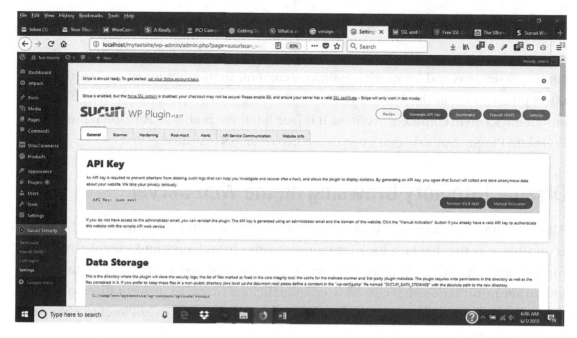

Figure 7-13. Sucuri API key and other settings

Antivirus Plugins

Antivirus software protects against viruses, malware, and SQL injections that target the WordPress database. It is recommended to use an antivirus plugin to scan a WordPress website for these intrusions. The Security, Antivirus, and Firewall (SAF) plugin by Smart Security Labs Technologies is free and provides antivirus file and security scanning and more to keep a website secure. With all plugins, it is important to make sure that they are compatible with a website's version of WordPress and review the number of times it has been downloaded. It is also a good idea to pay attention to when it was last updated. If it has not been updated in a while, it probably is not a good idea to use it.

Antispam Plugins

Another area of concern for an online store is spam comments. Spammers love to flood comment sections and forms with malicious content. To monitor for spam, WordPress offers plugins such as the Antispam plugin. The Antispam plugin by WebVitaly blocks automatic spam in comment sections. It is free, but there is also an Antispam Pro Premium Plugin available that extends the free version's features.

Disable Directory Browsing on the Web Server

Allowing directory browsing on your web server is not a good security idea. This is another way that hackers look for vulnerabilities in websites and execute brute force attacks. It is also a way for others to gain unauthorized access to files, images, and other information that can be used in malicious ways. To prevent directory browsing, connect to your web host via FTP or log in through the cPanel to change the permission.

Limiting User Permissions

For an online store, there might be many people working to help launch and maintain the store. WordPress makes it easy to create users and assign them roles. It is a good practice to assign the appropriate permission to a user's role to prevent unauthorized or accidental changes to content (Figure 7-14).

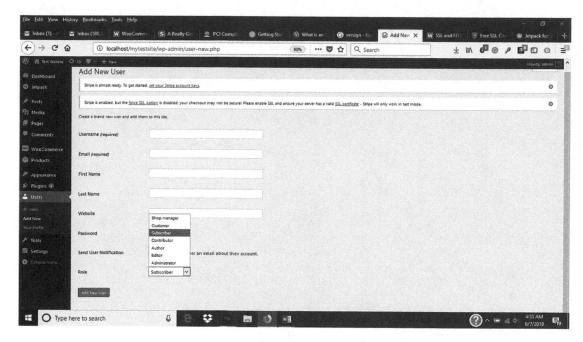

Figure 7-14. *Choosing a user role when adding a new user*

Privacy Policy

Visitors to a website have come to expect a privacy policy to be available at the bottom of a website. A privacy policy informs visitors of how their information will be used by the website as well as protected. WordPress allows the ability to create a privacy page or link to an existing page from Settings ➤ Privacy.

Summary

Before launching an online store, security should be addressed to not only protect the store but also customers' information. WordPress and WooCommerce provide many options to make this as easy as possible. Once security measures are implemented, they should be frequently monitored and reviewed so that any changes can be immediately implemented. The next chapter will explore some of the many options for testing an online store before it is launched.

CHAPTER 8

Testing Your Online Store

In the previous chapter, the importance of securing an online store was discussed along with practical ways to implement security. When implementing security, it should always be a top priority because not only is it a legal obligation, but also consumers expect companies that they conduct business with to protect their personal and financial information. Companies who do not comply with the latest security measures can quickly lose customers as well as go out of business. Depending on the business's size, the consequences can be devastating.

Before a company launches an online store, it is imperative that it is properly and thoroughly tested. Typically, testing is the last phase of a project that is done before an online store is launched. In an effort to launch a store by its deadline, some aspects of testing might be inadvertently overlooked. Depending on the severity of the issues discovered during testing, additional time and money could be required, which could delay the store's launch.

Testing helps companies feel confident that consumers will have a positive shopping experience. It does not mean that customers will not experience any errors because customers might follow a shopping path that was not initially tested. Testing allows companies an opportunity to correct any errors before customers discover them as well as ensure that the store works as designed and expected. It also helps consumers not only have a good shopping experience but also build credibility and trust with a company's brand. Nothing is more frustrating for consumers than to have a difficult time navigating an online store or an even difficult time checking out once they have placed items in their shopping cart.

A good first impression not only begins with the aesthetics of an online store but also the entire shopping experience from beginning to end. Putting in the initial time and work to test an online store can help companies ensure that the potential sales revenue can be achieved. By following some simple guidelines provided in this chapter, an online store can be tested to help provide a memorable customer experience.

© Lisa Sims 2018
L. Sims, *Building Your Online Store With WordPress and WooCommerce*,
https://doi.org/10.1007/978-1-4842-3846-2_8

Choosing a Testing Strategy

When it comes to testing an online store, many options are available. However, all options might not be a good fit for a particular online store in terms of complexity and ease of execution. Regardless of the strategy chosen, it is important to choose a strategy that not only works but is also flexible enough to address unanticipated areas of concern. Let's take a look at some testing strategies that can work for validating most online stores.

Testers

Once all the product, shipping, payment, and order confirmation information has been set up in WooCommerce, it is important to test the online store. Testing can either be done by an individual or by a group of individuals. It is a good practice to use a group of individuals for testing as opposed to an individual. A group of individuals can discover issues that might be otherwise missed by an individual. Remember the saying, "Two sets of eyes are better than one"? It definitely applies to this situation. When choosing a group of individuals, it is good to select individuals who do not have a technical background because they can model how potential visitors would use the online store, which will provide additional insight. Family and friends can make good testers. Other testers can be found for a fee by using third-party websites such as www.usertesting.com, www.userlytics.com, and www.enroll.com.

Product Images

What good is a product or service if consumers cannot visualize it? With online stores, the ability to physically touch and see it are not available, so every effort must be made to duplicate it. Consumers want and need an idea of what they are potentially buying. When testing the online store, make sure that all product images are properly displayed. It is also good to make sure that the images are of good size and quality. When adding product images, it is a best practice to make sure that images are not too large in size, which can slow down the page load time speed and potentially hurt a store's search engine optimization (SEO) efforts on sites such as Google. For example, as of July 9, 2018, Google's Speed Update algorithm has been incorporated into mobile search results as a search ranking factor.[1] No specifics were given as to how Google determines which websites are considered fast or slow or the percentage of websites that will be affected.

---

[1]https://searchengineland.com/google-speed-update-is-now-being-released-to-all-users-301657

For products and services, verify that the full product or service image along with the small thumbnail image displays correctly. WooCommerce recommends a minimum width of 800 pixels and a height of 800 pixels for product (or service) images because they will display well for the main/featured image, catalog image, and thumbnail image.[2] It also recommends larger-sized images for items that contain great detail, but keep in mind the larger the file size, the longer page load speed that affects search engine rankings. When adding products or services, these images can easily be omitted so it is always a good idea to verify that every product or service that needs an image has one associated with it. It is also a good practice to use white or light backgrounds for product or service images along with square or portrait orientation to make it easier for buyers to see products' details. Likewise, it is a good idea to verify any copyrights associated with any images used for the online store.

Product Descriptions

In the same manner that product images are reviewed, products and services descriptions should be reviewed. Each sellable item should have a short and long description. Not only should the descriptions exist, but they should also be free from spelling and grammatical errors. Spelling and grammatical errors can make an online store appear unprofessional and sloppy. Like it or not, people tend to judge a website by the quality of its content. Misspelled words can convey a lack of attention to detail, which could cause concern for potential customers. To avoid this, product descriptions can be checked by either manually viewing them or copying them into a word processing program such as Microsoft Word and spell checking them.

Product Categories

To help consumers easily find the products that they want, categories should be used. When reviewing online store categories, make sure that they are descriptive and describe the products or services that are assigned to them. Consumers do not like to guess what products make up a category, so make it as simple as possible to locate products. Lastly, the product categories should be free from spelling errors.

---

[2]https://docs.woocommerce.com/document/adding-product-images-and-galleries/

SSL Implemented

Even if customers place items in their shopping cart, it does not mean that they will buy them. If they do not see signs that an SSL certificate has been implemented, some might not trust an online store with their personal and credit card information, particularly if a store is relatively new. Most modern web browsers such as Google Chrome will label websites without SSL for the entire website as nonsecure, which could affect potential customers' perception of an online store. To help ease potential customers' fears, it is still a good practice to check that SSL is implemented by adding items to the shopping cart and proceeding to the checkout (Figure 8-1).

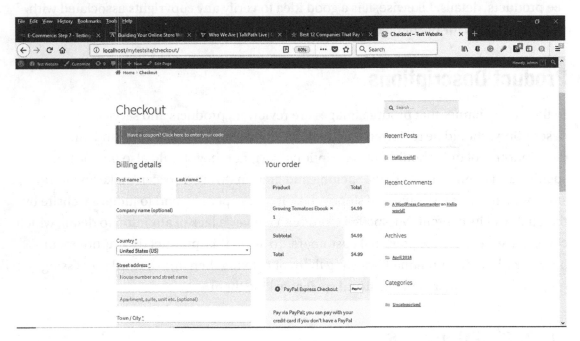

Figure 8-1. *Testing the SSL in the checkout process*

The address bar should either show "https" or display green. Likewise, a lock icon should be displayed either at the bottom of the browser window or in the address bar. Even though setting up SSL certificates was explained in Chapter 8, it is still good to test it for your business's peace of mind and that of your potential customers. To force SSL at checkout, make sure that the Force secure checkout option is checked on the Advanced Tab of the WooCommerce ➤ Settings menu (Figure 8-2).

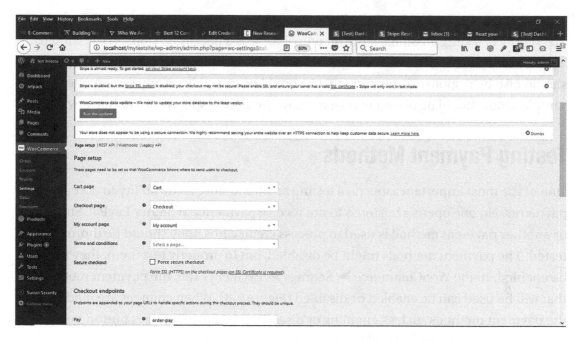

Figure 8-2. *Forcing secure checkout on the Advanced Tab*

Sample Data Deleted

If any of the sample products were added into WooCommerce during the initial store setup, they should be deleted. Since these products and services are not a part of a company's inventory, potential customers should not see them and mistakenly try to order them. Likewise, any sample posts and images should also be deleted. By deleting unused items, it frees up storage space within the WordPress MySQL database, which can help reduce the database size and improve database performance.

Mobile Device Testing

Since more consumers are using their mobile devices to make online purchases, it is important to make sure that an online store not only displays correctly but also functions correctly. According to new research, consumers in the 18–29 age range are 84 percent more likely to use a mobile device when shopping online, followed by the 30–44 age range at 74 percent.[3]

---

[3]https://www.prnewswire.com/news-releases/new-research-finds-consumers-use-mobile-devices-for-product-information-whether-shopping-in-store-or-at-home-300434981.html

Since iOS and Android mobile devices are the most prevalently used in the marketplace, testing an online store on one of these is a necessity. Consumers should be able to easily navigate and make purchases from the online store. The online store should also be responsive, meaning that it should be viewable on any screen size. A sample order should be placed to observe how the store responds on mobile devices.

Testing Payment Methods

One of the most important aspects of testing an online store is the ability to accept payments. No one opens a business to not receive payments. Whether PayPal, Stripe, or another payment method is used to process credit cards, they should be thoroughly tested. The payment methods might be disabled, but to properly test them, they need to be enabled. In the WooCommerce ➤ Settings ➤ Payments Tab, the payment methods that will be used can be enabled or disabled (Figure 8-3). When changes are made to the payment methods such as enabling or disabling, the Save Changes button must be clicked. Otherwise, changes will not be saved.

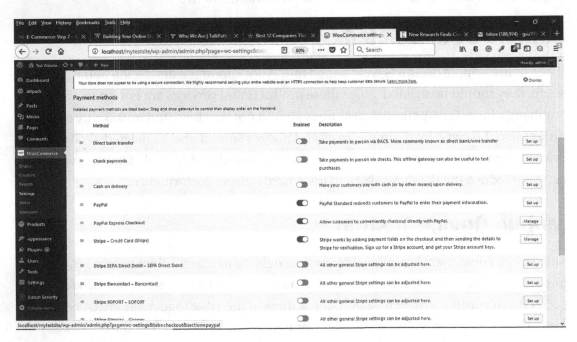

Figure 8-3. *Enabling payment methods in WooCommerce*

PayPal

If PayPal is used, it will need to be set up or managed (Figure 8-4).

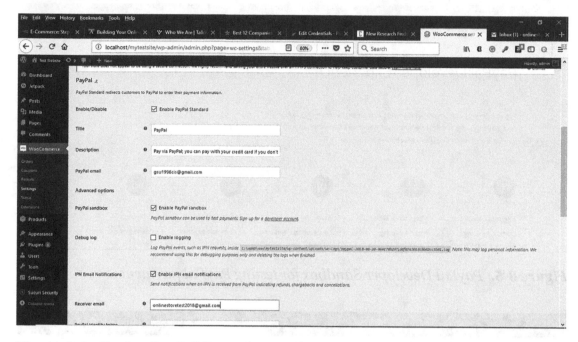

Figure 8-4. *Testing PayPal For Payment Processing*

Whether PayPal, PayPal Express, or both or used, they need to be properly tested. Using PayPal takes customers to the PayPal website after a completed checkout to make their payment. Customers are directed back to the online store after the PayPal checkout. Since payments are processed on the PayPal server, an Instant Payment Notification (IPN) must be sent to an online store, indicating success or failure for completed orders. As a result, orders can sometimes not be completed correctly, which is why IPN's are sometimes considered to be unreliable. PayPal Express, however, does not use IPN's. Although customers are directed to the PayPal website, they do not pay there. They approve their purchase and are returned to the online store to complete their payment and checkout with a hidden token. The hidden token is used to submit final payment to PayPal. Payment is still processed on PayPal's servers, but checkout happens at the online store. PayPal does offer a developer sandbox that can be used to test the PayPal payment process. A developer account is needed (Figure 8-5). It can be created by clicking the Login Dashboard button (Figure 8-6). Once a Developer Account is created, test orders can be generated and the payments viewed within the Developer Sandbox.

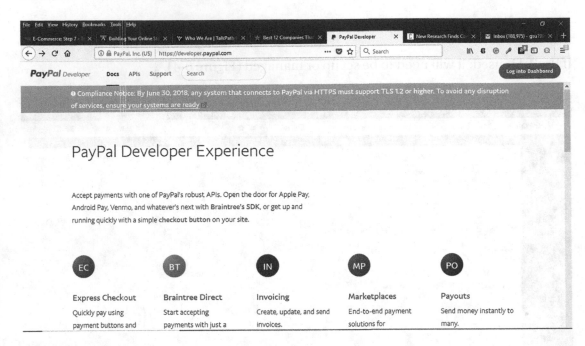

Figure 8-5. *PayPal Developer Sandbox for testing PayPal payments*

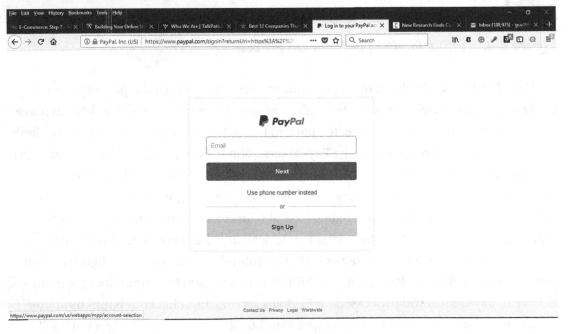

Figure 8-6. *PayPal Developer Sandbox Sign-Up Page*

To test your PayPal Checkout Integration within the Sandbox, a token has to be generated from within the Sandbox (Figure 8-7) . Within the Developer Sandbox, a maximum of five credentials can be created. Once a credential is selected, an access token is generated, and different currencies can be selected for testing purposes (Figure 8-8).

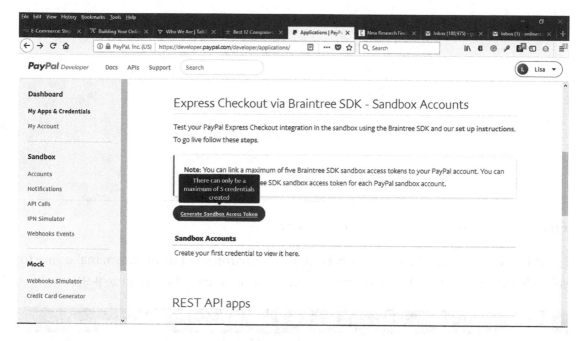

Figure 8-7. *Generating Sandbox Access Tokens Within PayPal Sandbox*

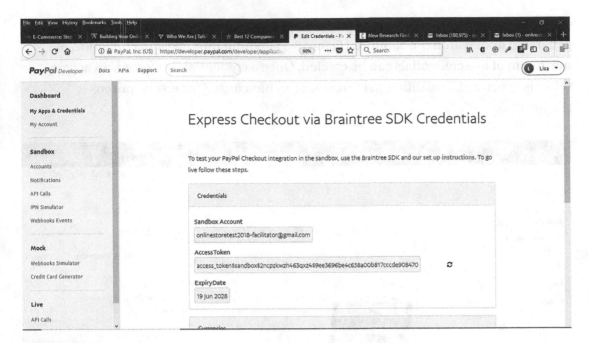

Figure 8-8. *Sandbox Account Access Token*

When testing PayPal Express Checkout in the Environment drop-down, make sure to select Sandbox. Once testing is completed, make sure to select Live (Figure 8-9).

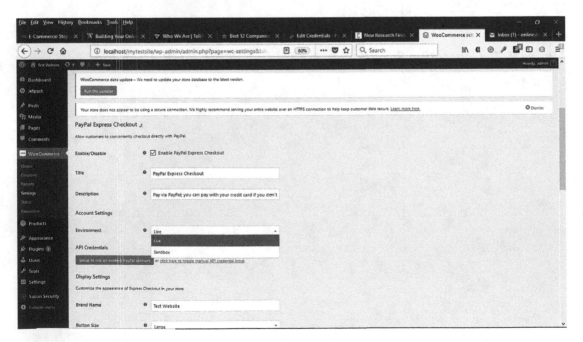

Figure 8-9. *Selecting the Sandbox for testing*

The PayPal Developer Sandbox account information can be entered in the Payment module on the Payment Tab. It is also important to verify that all the information is correctly listed. Documentation is also available within the Developer Sandbox to further assist with PayPal testing.

Stripe

Stripe is another payment method that can be used to process credit card payments. To use Stripe, an account must be set up at `https://dashboard.stripe.com/register` (Figure 8-10).

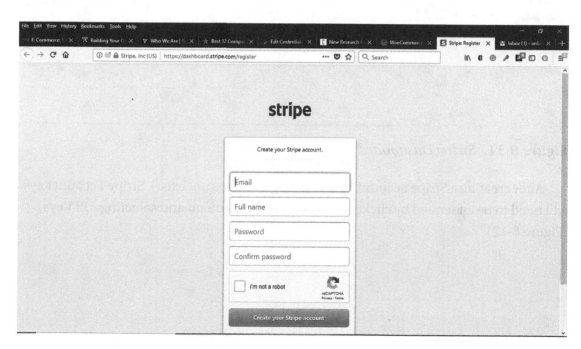

Figure 8-10. *Registering for a Stripe account*

Once an account is created, the dashboard will be displayed (Figure 8-11).

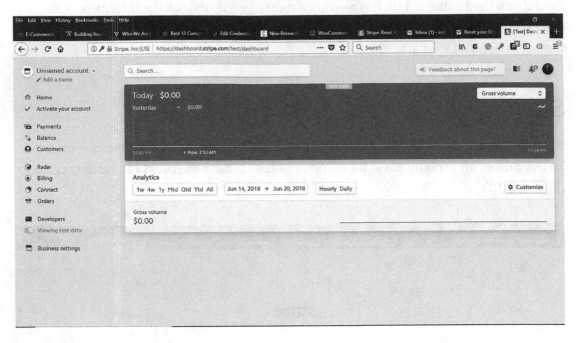

Figure 8-11. *Stripe Dashboard*

After creating a Stripe account (if an existing one does not exist), Stripe account keys will need to be generated by clicking on the Developers menu and selecting API Keys (Figure 8-12).

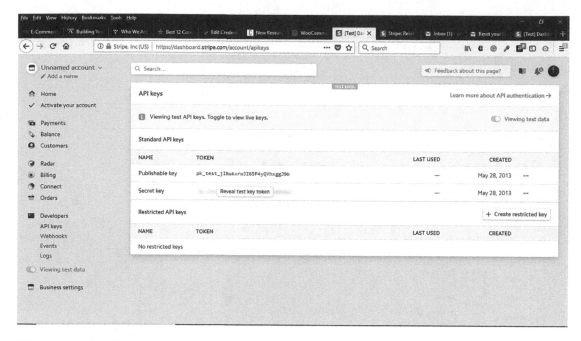

Figure 8-12. *Generating Stripe API Keys*

Click on the Business Settings menu to complete the company information. On the Relay menu within the Business Settings menu, verify that test mode is selected (Figure 8-13). On the Customer Email menu within the Business Settings, complete the information that will be displayed to the customer once a successful order has been placed. After it has been verified that the Test Mode has been selected, enter the Test Publishable Key and Test Secret Key that were generated into the WooCommerce ➤ Settings ➤ Payment Tab for Stripe. All remaining information needs to be verified for correctness. Once it has been verified, proceed to place and order using Stripe, and keep the Stripe dashboard open to verify the test transaction.

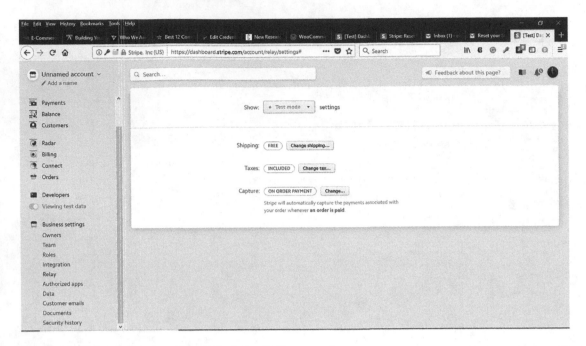

Figure 8-13. *Selecting Test Mode in Relay section*

Accounts & Privacy

Within the WooCommerce ➤ Settings ➤ Accounts & Privacy, verify that a privacy page is listed along with a registration privacy and checkout privacy policy. Consumers want to know how their information will be used on a website and expect to see this information listed. Also, review the Guest Checkout and Account Creation options to make certain that they are correct.

Emails

Once orders are placed, the necessary personnel need to be notified so that orders can be fulfilled. On the WooCommerce ➤ Settings ➤ Email Tab, the emails of the order fulfillment team need to be placed here (Figure 8-14).

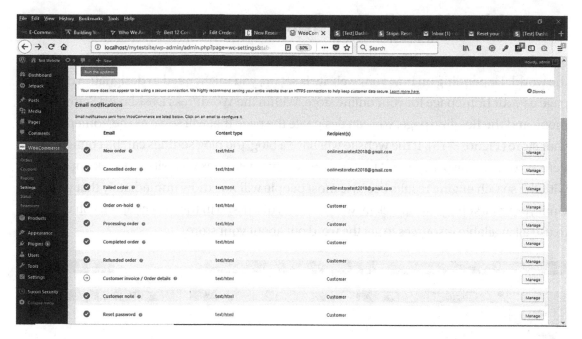

Figure 8-14. *Email notification settings for the order process*

Testing Virtual Products

For those products that are downloadable, the download process must be tested. The download link that is emailed to the customer needs to be tested to make sure that the product can be downloaded without error.

Logging Debugging Information

During testing, debugging information might be obtained to help pinpoint an error and added to the WooCommerce debug log. However, once the store launches, this information should be deleted because it can consume space on the web server needed for the store.

Launching Your Online Store

Now that your online store has been tested and errors corrected, it is now time to launch it to the world. Depending on how your website is set up, you might need to designate a different page as your homepage for your online store. Within the WordPress Dashboard Settings menu and the Reading page, you can designate the page that will serve as the homepage for your store (Figure 8-15). If the website will have a blog, the blog settings can be configured here as well. It is also important to let the search engines index your site so that it appears with the search engine results because most people will not know immediately that you exist. Until your marketing efforts kick in, which will be discussed in the next chapter, you will need to use all available resources to get the word out about your store.

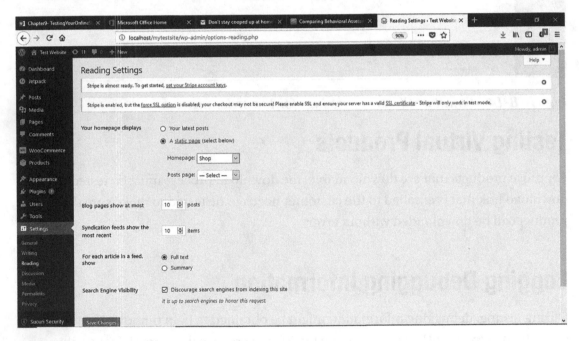

Figure 8-15. *Selecting the homepage on the Reading Settings page*

Summary

Testing an online store is imperative before it launches. It helps to prevent customers from experiencing errors during their shopping experience. Not all errors will be caught, but at least companies can rest assured that they did their due diligence before launching the store to the public. The next chapter will focus on how to market an online store once it's launched.

CHAPTER 9

Marketing Your Online Store

The last chapter addressed various ways to test an online store for potential errors before it launches. Properly testing an online store with multiple users is considered a best practice and helps catch errors that might be missed by a single user. Once all testing has been completed and all errors corrected, the online store can be launched.

Once an online store is launched, many store owners think they can take it easy and wait for orders to come in because the hard work has been done. Some also have the Kevin Costner vision from the movie, *Field of Dreams*: If you build it, they will come. They envision their online stores being flooded with consumers who will purchase their products or services. However, this could not be further from the truth. If marketing has not taken place before the store launches, how will the target audience know the store exists? They will not. Marketing is the key to notifying the world that any type of store exists. Without a well-planned marketing strategy that is frequently reviewed, it is possible to go out of business sooner rather than later.

Marketing Strategy

After an online store launches, it can be common practice to start planning a marketing strategy, but as stated in Chapter 2, if you fail to plan, you plan to fail. In marketing, one of the most basic concepts is the 4's of Marketing: product, price, promotion, and place. Through the book, you have learned how to address the place, product, and price, but now it is time to consider the online store's promotion. It is a good idea to start asking some of the five W's and H questions concerning promotion:

- Who will be in charge of the promotion campaigns?

- What promotion techniques or methods will be used?

© Lisa Sims 2018
L. Sims, *Building Your Online Store With WordPress and WooCommerce*,
https://doi.org/10.1007/978-1-4842-3846-2_9

- When will promotions begin?

- Where will the promotions take place?

- Why is promotion important?

- How will the promotion take place?

As entrepreneurs and small business owners, it can be easy to create a marketing plan on the fly. It can generate some short-term sales and success, but it will not prepare a business for long-term sales growth and success. To be effective, a marketing strategy has to consider a business's marketing budget along with the free and paid promotion resources that are available. How much should a business budget for marketing? A common rule of thumb is to spend 5 percent of a company's total revenue on marketing, but if for a new online business, chances are that no revenue has been made. In this case, it would be better to focus on the free promotion/marketing resources until there is sufficient revenue to budget for paid resources that have a proven and positive return on investment.

Free and Inexpensive Marketing Resources

Until your online store becomes profitable, conserving money should be a top priority. With so many effective and inexpensive marketing resources available, why not start with them first? Let's take a look at some.

Social Media

Social media has changed the way the world communicates and collaborates with each other. Spredfast.com reported that as of 2018, 37 percent of the world's population, which is the equivalent of 2.8 billion people, use social media.[1] With so many different social media platforms available to use for free with only an investment of time and effort, it only makes sense to take advantage of them. However, which ones should a business choose? According to a 2018 Pew Research Center survey, U.S. adults primarily use YouTube (73 percent) and Facebook (68 percent) online or on their cellphones, followed by Instagram (35 percent).[2] What about the other social media platforms?

---

[1]https://www.spredfast.com/social-media-tips/social-media-demographics-current
[2]http://www.pewinternet.org/2018/03/01/social-media-use-in-2018/

The other social media platforms such as Twitter, Pinterest, Snapchat, and LinkedIn are used but with smaller numbers and different age demographics. Does this mean a business should only focus its marketing efforts on YouTube and Facebook and forget about the others? No it does not. It simply means that YouTube and Facebook should automatically be included in a business's marketing efforts along with those platforms whose demographics match up with its target audience. Let's take a look at some of these platforms and how they can be used.

YouTube

When most people hear the name YouTube, online videos immediately come to their minds. Brandwatch.com reports that YouTube is "the world's second largest search engine and third most visited site after Google and Facebook."[3] It also reported that 400 hours of video are uploaded to YouTube every minute and over 1 billion hours of videos are watched a day. With these types of numbers, it is a no-brainer that a business should have a YouTube channel for their videos. Advances in technology have made it possible to create great videos inexpensively and edit them using mobile devices and mobile apps. During these videos, a business could provide demonstrations, commercials, or other engaging content about their products or services and reference their online store for viewers to visit. It is also a good idea to include a link to the online store in the Links section of a YouTube's About Page.

Facebook

Following closely behind YouTube, millennials and Generation X are the top Facebook users. As of December 2017, Facebook estimated that it averaged 1.4 billion users as daily active users.[4] Not only do people enjoy sharing photos, videos, and other content, but they also ask for recommendations using the Facebook recommendation feature. One common free way that businesses can use Facebook to promote their products or services is via a business or fan page. By creating a business page, a business can add a shop now button on their page that can take visitors directly to their online store. The page will also allow a business to promote its products or services via images, videos, and more. Another Facebook feature that is good for promotion is Facebook

---

[3]https://www.brandwatch.com/blog/39-youtube-stats/
[4]https://www.cnn.com/2014/02/11/world/facebook-fast-facts/index.html

Live. Facebook Live allows Facebook users to broadcast real-time video sessions from any Internet-connected mobile device and actively engage with their audience. These live broadcasts can be shot from anywhere and at any time and can last up to four hours. Once the broadcasts are over, they can be saved to a Facebook Page or Profile for others to view who might not have been able to view the live session. Facebook Live is an inexpensive way to not only increase a business's followers but also promote new products or services or specials.

Twitter

How much can be said using 140 characters? Quite a lot. Twitter can be used to send out tweets about the launch of a new business, new products or services, or any other helpful relationship-building information. For posts that are more than 140 characters long, URL shorteners such as bit.ly can be used to shorten a URL so that it can stay with the 140 characters limit as well as provide more analytic information concerning who engaged with the tweet. Similar to Facebook, Twitter also allows live videos to be created and shared to the Twitter stream and be searchable on Periscope. Periscope is Twitter's live streaming website.

Instagram

Instagram is another social media platform that can help market an online business. Once a business account is created, posts can be made with images or video created that can be shared with potential buyers. Instagram also provides insights to learn about followers or create promotions to grow a business. Within a user's account profile, a URL can be added to help potential buyers locate their online store.

LinkedIn

Businesses and business professionals use LinkedIn to connect with other businesses and business professionals. LinkedIn, owned by Microsoft, claims to have over 500 billion users, so why would a business professional or company not utilize the social network?[5] With features similar to Facebook such as newsfeed, posts, ads, and groups,

---

[5]http://fortune.com/2017/04/24/linkedin-users/

LinkedIn can increase not only a company's brand but also its followers. Similar to creating a Facebook page, companies can create a free LinkedIn company page that can be used to tell LinkedIn users about the company and products and services (Figure 9-1). With a LinkedIn company page, companies can add a logo and header image, company description, company website URL, publish and share content, and more.

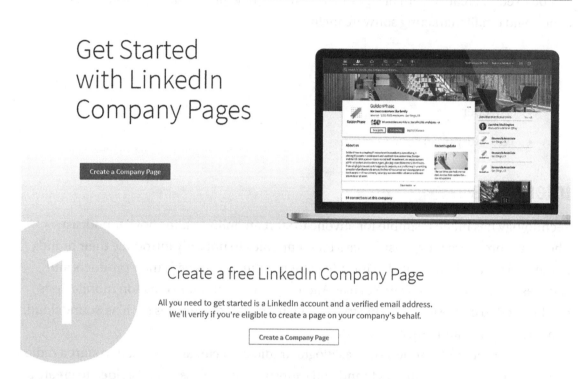

Figure 9-1. *Creating a free LinkedIn Company Page*

Snapchat

Depending on the target audience, Snapchat could be a good social media tool to use to promote an online store. A Snapchat story can consist of a photo or video that can be shared with the world. These stories last 24 hours before they are removed from a person's Snapchat feed. Creating Snapchat stories with special discounts and coupons is a good way to attract visitors to the store.

E-newsletter

E-newsletters can be a great, inexpensive way to keep customers informed of a company's latest happenings such as events, new products or services, sales, and more. In the case of a new business, it can be a good idea to allow potential customers to sign up on its website for its e-newsletter. Free email marketing software such as MailChimp can be used to create an email sign-up form that can be placed on a website or blog. Other paid email marketing software include:

- Constant Contact
- Drip
- Aweber
- Get Response

Interviews

Technology has made it simple for anyone to start an online radio show or podcast. These resources are inexpensive ways for companies to not only introduce their brands to their target audience but also introduce their online stores with their products and services to the world. Software such as Audacity and other audio creation mobile apps can be used to create an audio file that can be uploaded to websites such as Soundcloud.com, libsyn.com, and others.

Paid Internet radio shows such as Blogtalkradio.com can also be used to start a radio show and increase a business's brand and exposure. Not only is it a good idea to create a radio show but to also reach out to different online shows whose theme fits nicely with a company's products or services and also have a nice size audience.

Press Releases

A press release is an inexpensive way to inform the public about something that has or will take place that is considered newsworthy. Some examples include the opening of a new business, community event, and others. Since it is not a paid advertisement, it tends to have more credibility than traditional ads and appears as a typical news story. Not only can a properly written press release be published in a newspaper but also help generate the interest for a news story. A press release can either appear in print media sources such as newspapers or online sources such as blogs, search engines, and online news sites. Printed press releases can be harder to get the attention of a reporter particularly if it is not written in an interesting or engaging manner. A typical press release answers the 5 W's (who, what, where, why, and when) questions. Press release templates can be located within Microsoft Word as well as searching for them on Google. Freelance press release writers can also be found on freelance websites such as fiverr.com and elance.com.

Since launching an online store can be written in a newsworthy way, it would be perfect for a press release. A business would have to contact the media outlets it plans to target to get the appropriate media contacts information along with the preferred submission method (i.e., email, fax, mail). Free online press release websites are good for businesses to use to help their target audience locate them in search engines, blogs, and news sites. Although paid press release distribution websites such as prweb.com are available, it is always a good practice to start with the free resources before spending any money. A few of the free online press release websites worth looking into are:

- Free-press-release.com

- Pr.com

- Newswiretoday.com

- I-newswire.com

- Express-press-release.com

- Clickpress.com

- 24-7pressrelease.com

Custom Images

Most people have short attention spans and prefer visual content such as videos and images as opposed to reading text. Creating custom infographics using photography editing mobile apps such as Camly. ImageQuote, and PicLab, and free software such as Canva.com can help create professional-looking infographics and sales graphics for the online store that can include the online store's URL. Once created, these images can be shared on other social media platforms.

Company Phone Message

With all the talk about social media and videos, it is easy to forget about something as simple as a company's phone greeting. The phone greeting is a great opportunity to tell callers about the newly launched online store as well as its URL.

Coupons and Discounts

Who does not like to save money? Everyone loves to save money, including potential customers. If coupon codes were not created during the initial setup of the online store, begin to create some coupon codes. These coupon codes can be shared on social media platforms such as Facebook, Twitter, Snapchat, and Instagram to name a few. Coupons provide an incentive for consumers to purchase a product or service while saving money.

Blogging

Who does not have a blog these days? Advances in blogging platforms have made it easy and fast for anyone to create a blog. The benefit of blogs is that people can blog about their interests and easily share those thoughts with the world who can also share those thoughts with their online network. Since blogs are updated more frequently than regular websites, they help increase search engine rankings.

Launching an online store provides enough new and fresh blog content to not only peek curiosity but also attract followers and visitors. Since your online store is already built on WordPress, blogging should not be a problem. Oftentimes, people worry that they will not have time to blog. Not a problem! WordPress allows blog posts to be scheduled, which is convenient and can fit within the busiest of schedules.

Pinterest

Pinterest is another social network that can be used to develop a company's brand and following. It is estimated to have over 200 million active monthly users who are mostly female. According to Pew Research, roughly 31 percent of Internet users use Pinterest.[6] These users share images and videos by "pinning" them to their virtual boards or others'

---

[6]http://www.pewinternet.org/2016/11/11/social-media-update-2016/

boards similar to bulletin boards of the past. People tend to search Pinterest similar to Google for items of interest and to discover new brands. With 35 percent of Pinterest users having an annual income of over $75,000, they can afford to make purchases.[7] Another good thing about Pinterest is that its pins are considered evergreen and are repined over 11 times, which can increase a brand's exposure. Not only can sharing product images or videos help increase your online store's brand, but also sharing and saving others' pins can help your online store gain needed attention.

Paid Social Media Ads

Depending on which social media platforms a business uses, they all offer some type of paid ads. These ads can be customized to fit a business's demographic needs as well as its budget. For example, Facebook allows paid ads to be created and purchased based on a budget amount as well as demographic information. Once the ad information has been entered, Facebook will provide information on how many people the ad will reach. It also allows tracking of the ad campaign for the ad duration. Other social media sites such as Twitter, Instagram, LinkedIn, and more offer this option as well. Which one you choose depends on your target audience as well as your budget.

Summary

Marketing an online store is a continuous job that must be reviewed frequently. To truly be effective and receive good, positive results, consistent marketing strategies must be used. It is also a good idea to review the marketing budget to see how much is available for marketing purposes. If a budget does not exist, it is good to start out with free marketing resources. When using a good mix of marketing strategies, a good return on investment can be achieved.

---

[7]https://blog.hootsuite.com/pinterest-statistics-for-business/

CHAPTER 10

Maintaining Your Online Store

Chapter 9 discussed various strategies for marketing an online store. Without a well-planned marketing strategy, it can be difficult for potential buyers to know an online store exists as well as for store owners to achieve some of their short-term and long-term goals. No matter how great a product selection an online store might have, marketing is still one of the key components to any successful business's success.

Now that your online store has launched, it has to be maintained. Although there are certain aspects of the online store that can operate on autopilot, it still needs to be maintained to make sure that it is operating correctly and efficiently and producing the anticipated goals and revenue. Sometimes it is easier and less expensive to correct an issue by being proactive rather than being reactive. In this chapter, we will take a look at some tips and strategies to help maintain your online store to produce a win-win for both store owners and customers.

Updating WooCommerce

Within the WordPress Dashboard, WooCommerce will indicate whether or not an update is available (Figure 10-1). Making sure that WooCommerce is up to date helps protect your online store from vulnerabilities and security breaches that have been discovered that could pose potential problems or threats to not only your store's security but also your customer's information. Likewise, it makes sure that your store is using the latest version of WooCommerce, which might include new features that can enhance your store as well as shoppers' experiences.

© Lisa Sims 2018
L. Sims, *Building Your Online Store With WordPress and WooCommerce*,
https://doi.org/10.1007/978-1-4842-3846-2_10

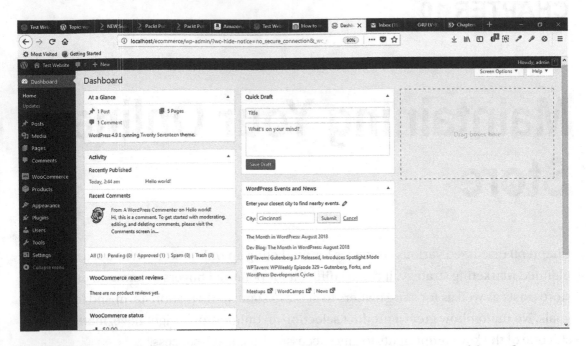

Figure 10-1. *Updating WooCommerce through the WordPress Dashboard*

Before applying any updates to WooCommerce, it is a good practice to perform a backup to prevent any data loss or corruption of the WooCommerce database that organizes and stores your store's information and key WordPress content such as themes, plugins, and other content located in the wp-content folder on your web server.

Updating WordPress

When a new version of WordPress is released, it is crucial that your version is updated. This helps your website stay up to date and protects it from security and bugs concerns. Within the WordPress Dashboard, a message will appear near the top indicating that an update is available. WordPress can be updated via the WordPress Dashboard by clicking on Updates. If nothing is displayed, try clicking the Check Again button to see if there is one available (Figure 10-2).

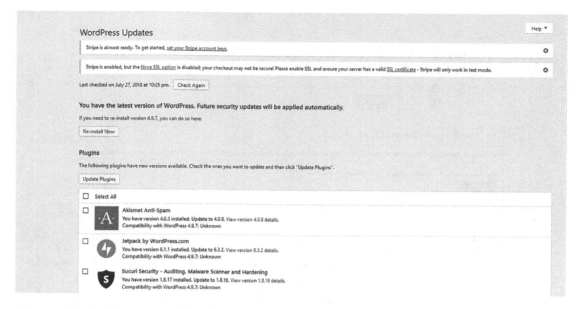

Figure 10-2. *Updating WordPress via the WordPress Dashboard*

Updates can also be done manually via FTP or configured via most web hosts to be updated automatically. Prior to updating WordPress, be sure to perform a backup of your existing WordPress files by using a free or premium backup plugin such as:

- JetPack

- Backup Buddy

- Updraft Plus

- BackWpUP

Updating Plugins

Plugins are constantly being updated to address bugs and security concerns or replace an outdated version. For the continual operation of your store, it is imperative that all plugins used in your store are not outdated. Outdated plugins could compromise your entire online store and cause it to not work correctly. Within the WordPress Dashboard Plugins Page, WordPress indicates which plugins need to be updated by providing a highlighted message (Figure 10-3).

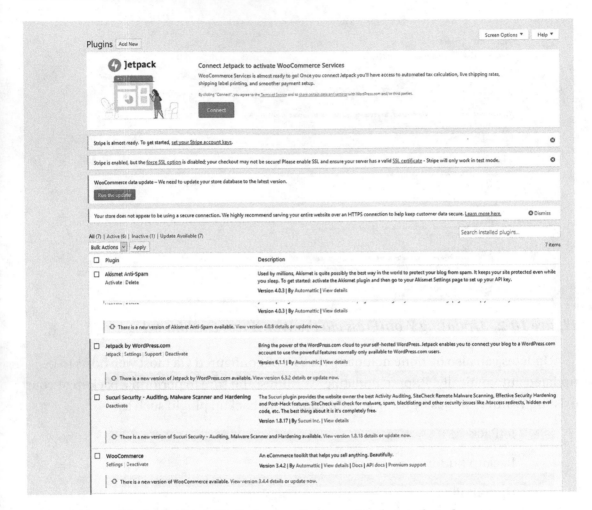

Figure 10-3. *Listing of installed plugins that need to be updated*

Updating WooCommerce Extensions

Upon initially installing WooCommerce, you either signed up for a WooCommerce.com account or postponed it to a later time. Within the WordPress Dashboard WooCommerce Page, you can purchase extensions that provide additional features to your online store (Figure 10-4). Some of those extension include:

- Memberships

- Subscriptions

- Bookings

- Product Add-Ons

- Checkout Add-On

- Cart Reports

- Smart Coupons

- Follow-Up Emails

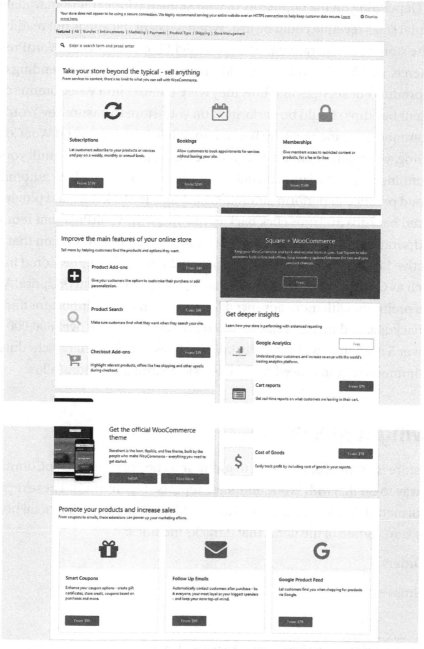

Figure 10-4. *WooCommerce extensions in the WordPress Dashboard*

Backing Up WordPress and WooCommerce

Regular backups are crucial to your store's success and bottom line. If your store malfunctions for any reason or you forget to renew your store's web hosting, your store could experience downtime in which prospects and repeat customers cannot make purchases. Depending on the popularity of your store, the longer it is unavailable, the more potential sales revenue could be lost. When a recent backup is not readily available to restore the store to an operational state, you might have to reinstall WordPress and WooCommerce, which can involve a considerable amount of time depending on the number of products or services and how they were entered into WooCommerce.

Consistent backups should be performed on your store to ensure key WordPress and WooCommerce components are backed up. While WordPress and WooCommerce are reinstalling, your store is offline, and you are losing potential sales until your store is up and running again. Backups can either be performed manually or automatically, but it is a good practice to perform automatic backups. JetPack is a good plugin to use for automated backups and one-click backup restores with VaultPress but requires a paid plan. UpdraftPlus offers a free restoration and backup plugin version that has over a million active installs. Once a backup has been scheduled, it can be stored in cloud services such as Google Drive, Dropbox, Amazon S3, or UpdraftPlus's UpdraftVault. It also offers a premium with more advanced features such as site duplicator and migrator, automatic backups, and more. Another option is BackWPup with over 600,000 active users and over 5 million downloads.[1] BackWPup allows backups to be scheduled or performed immediately and saved to cloud services similar to UpdraftPlus.

Reviewing Reports

Once your store is launched, you want to monitor its performance. WooCommerce provides a way to do this with WooCommerce reports (Figure 10-5). These reports provide information in numerical as well as graphical form on the financial health of your online store. Some of the items that it tracks includes:

- Orders
- Gross sales

---

[1] https://bloggingwizard.com/wordpress-backup-plugins/

- Net sales

- Items purchased

- Refunded orders

- Shipping charges

- Coupons used

Based on this information, you can monitor your online store's performance and make any necessary adjustments to your marketing efforts.

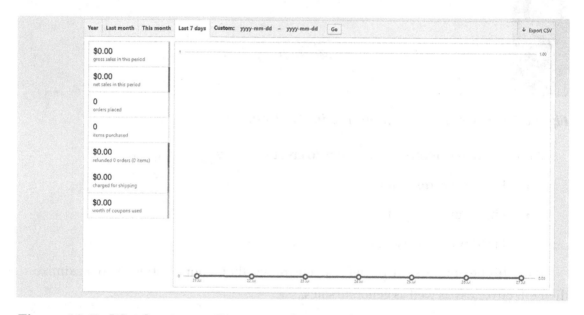

Figure 10-5. *WooCommerce Reports within WordPress Dashboard*

Coupons/Discounts

Whether your brand is already established before your online store launched or not, coupons can be a good marketing strategy to entice prospects to visit your online store (Figure 10-6). Who can resist saving money with a coupon? Coupons are not only good for attracting prospects but also encouraging repeat customers to visit and purchase items. These coupons can be given descriptive names and descriptions to help track their effectiveness in generating sales.

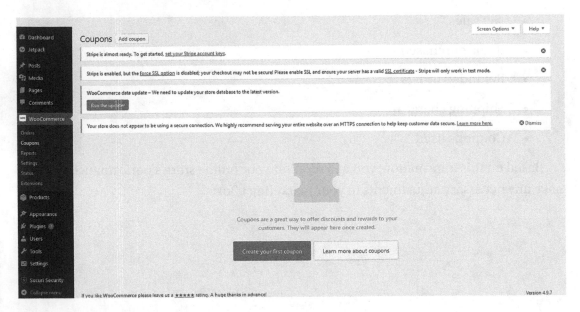

Figure 10-6. *Creating coupons within WooCommerce*

WooCommerce allows store owners to create three types of coupons:

- Percentage discount

- Fixed cart discount

- Fixed product discount

With this flexibility, store owners can customize their coupon strategy to maximize their effectiveness as well as generate sales.

Renewing Domain Name

Domain names are an important part of an online store's existence. It helps to build its brand. It is also one of the things people will remember about the store. Domain names have to be renewed for one to five years. Longer renewals help with search engine optimization because it shows that it will be around for a while. If not renewed, someone else can purchase the domain name, which will disrupt the operation of the store until another domain is purchased or repurchased from the domain buyer often at a much higher price. Automatic renewals with the chosen domain registrar are a good strategy to implement to prevent someone else from acquiring a store's domain name as well as an interruption in service.

Renewing Web Hosting

Besides not renewing a domain name, not renewing web hosting can cause an immediate disruption in the store's operation. Not only will this result in downtime and lost sales but also the possibility of re-creating the store if a recent backup is not available. It is a good idea to periodically check the expiration of the credit card that is on file with the web host (as well as the domain registrar) to make sure that it has not expired. An expired credit card can also result in a store's downtime. Also, it is good idea to renew web hosting automatically to prevent an interruption in service along with possible file loss and deletion. Believe it or not, it does happen and can happen to you.

Providing New Products

Once an online store has been in business for a while, store owners can review the sales reports and determine which products are the top sellers and update their product inventory. Based on this information, either more of these products can be introduced or new products in this category can be introduced to shoppers. These new products can also be introduced in the email newsletter sent to prospects and customers.

Orders

As orders are placed, they will be available in the Orders page of WooCommerce (Figure 10-7).

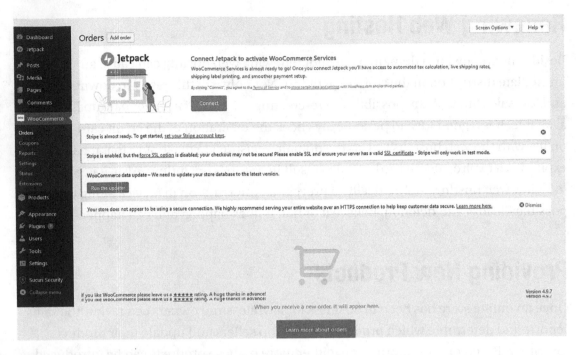

Figure 10-7. Orders within WooCommerce

Each order receives a status. According to the WooCommerce documentation, an order can have one of the following statuses:[2]

- Pending payment – Order received (unpaid).

- Failed – Payment failed or was declined (unpaid). Note that this status may not show immediately and instead show as Pending until verified (i.e., PayPal).

- Processing – Payment received, and stock has been reduced – the order is awaiting fulfillment. All product orders require processing, except those that only contain products that are both Virtual and Downloadable.

- Completed – Order fulfilled and complete – requires no further action.

- On-Hold – Awaiting payment – stock is reduced, but you need to confirm payment.

---

[2]https://docs.woocommerce.com/document/managing-orders/?utm_source=blankslate&utm_
medium=product&utm_content=ordersdoc&utm_campaign=woocommerceplugin

- Cancelled – Cancelled by an admin or the customer – no further action required. (Cancelling an order does not affect stock quantity by default.)

- Refunded – Refunded by an admin – no further action required.

By becoming familiar with these statuses, store owners can immediately identify when there is a problem with an order that might require attention. Downloading the WooCommerce app to a mobile device can also help store owners and store personnel stay abreast of sales and orders as they are received and know when it is time to fulfill them.

Google Analytics

How are people finding your online store? It is important to discover how prospects are finding your online store. If you cannot immediately answer this question, you might need some help. Google Analytics might be your answer. What is Google Analytics? Google Analytics provides detailed information about your website, its visitor demographics, and their actions while visiting your website and more. Compared to the standard web logs provided by web hosting companies, the amount and presentation of the information can provide valuable insight to help make improvements that can improve your store's bottom line. If you are using Google Ads, it provides information on the ad's performance. It is also free to use and is available as an app on Android and iOS devices.

To get started using Google Analytics, sign up for a free account at http:// analytics.google.com (Figure 10-8). To sign up, a Google account such as a Gmail account is needed.

Figure 10-8. *Signing up for Google Analytics*

After clicking the Sign-Up button, you will provide the requested form information and click the Get Tracking ID button (Figure 10-9). Accept the Google Analytics Terms of Service Agreement.

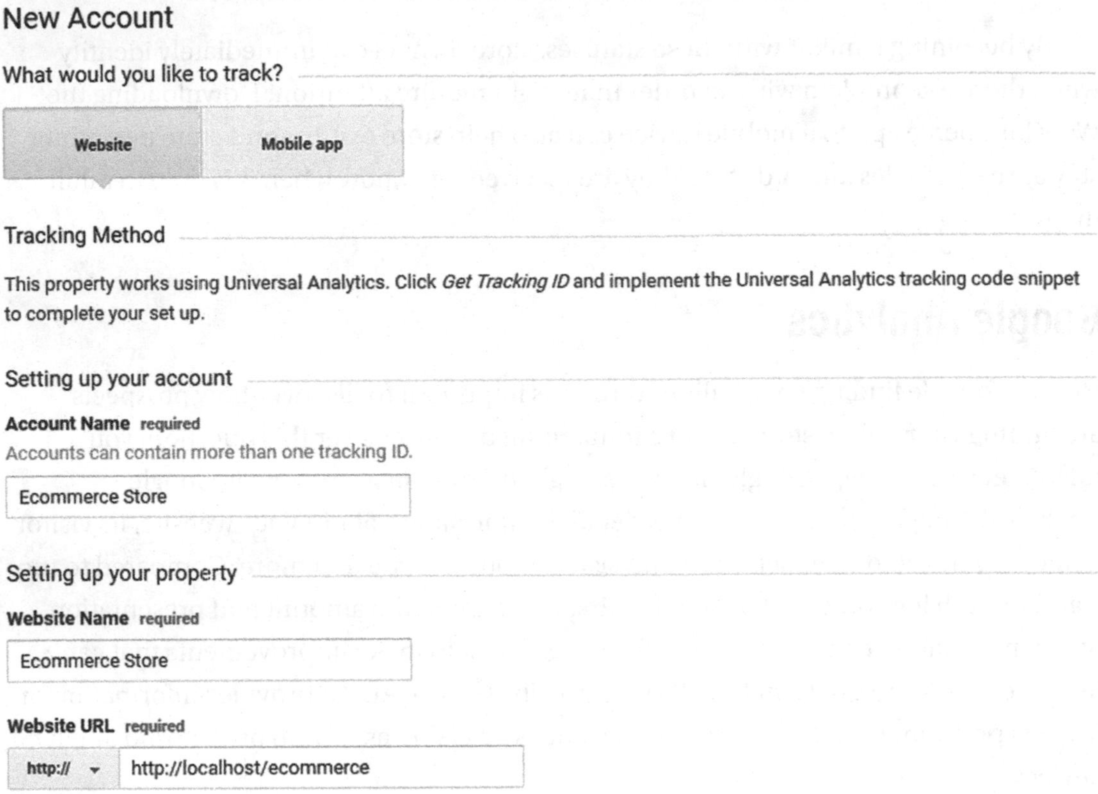

New Account

What would you like to track?

| Website | Mobile app |

Tracking Method

This property works using Universal Analytics. Click *Get Tracking ID* and implement the Universal Analytics tracking code snippet to complete your set up.

Setting up your account

Account Name required
Accounts can contain more than one tracking ID.

Ecommerce Store

Setting up your property

Website Name required

Ecommerce Store

Website URL required

http:// ▾ http://localhost/ecommerce

Figure 10-9. *Creating new Google Analytics account*

Once the tracking ID has been generated, the analytics can be viewed within Google Analytics or the tracking ID copied into one of the WordPress Google Analytics plugins such as Google Analytics for WordPress or Google Analytics Dashboard for WP that have been installed over a million times (Figure 10-10).

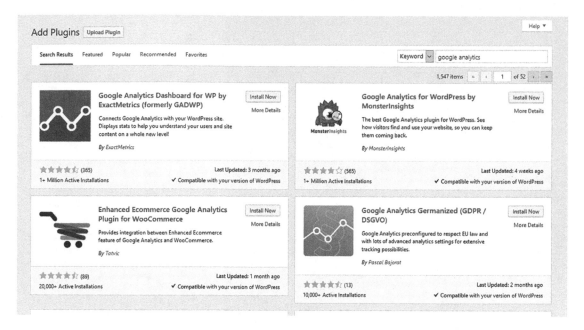

Figure 10-10. *Google Analytics plugins to help monitor website traffic*

Summary

Once an online store launches, the work does not end. It actually begins because the store must be maintained. Its success (and failure) depends on the amount of maintenance applied to help the store meet its short-term and long-term goals. By following these strategies, an online store can operate efficiently and provide a good customer shopping experience.

Index

A

Advanced Research Projects
Agency (ARPA), 3
Alibaba, 6
Amazon, 4–5, 8, 13, 16
Antispam plugin, 130
Antivirus software protects, 129
ARPANET, 3
Asynchronous JavaScript
and XML (AJAX), 71

B

Bankers Automated Clearing
Service (BACS), 45
Blogging, marketing, 156
Brainstorm, 57
Business.com, 6
Business-to-business (B2B), 4, 40
Business-to-consumer (B2C), 4, 7, 40

C

Cascading style sheet (CSS), 99
Certificate Authorities (CAs), 115, 117
Company phone message, 156
CompuServe, 4
Consumer behavior, 8
Consumers security, 113

Content management system (CMS), 11, 24
See also WordPress
Coupons, 156, 165–166
Cyber security, 44

D

Debugging information, 147
Discounts, 156, 165–166
Downloadable products, 104–106

E

eBay, 5–6, 13, 40
E-business, 2
E-commerce
in big and small businesses, 9
open source software, 11–12
purpose of, 9–10
consumer behavior and, 8
defined, 1–2
history, 3–4
purpose, 2
solutions, 42
traditional business model, 2
E-commerce strategy
budget, 18–19
creating, 16
inventory, 19–20
online store planning checklist

© Lisa Sims 2018
L. Sims, *Building Your Online Store With WordPress and WooCommerce*,
https://doi.org/10.1007/978-1-4842-3846-2

Y, Z

Printed in the United States
By Bookmasters